Beyond the Tool Belt

Blueprint for Making Money While You Sleep in the Blue-Collar World

BY

Kent A Kiess

BEYOND THE TOOL BELT

Copyright © 2023 by Kent Kiess.

All rights reserved. No part of this publication may be reproduced, distributed, or transmitted in any form or by any means, including photocopying, recording, or other electronic or mechanical methods, without the prior written permission of the author, except in the case of brief quotations embodied in critical reviews and certain other non-commercial uses permitted by copyright law.

This publication is designed to provide competent and reliable information. However, it is sold with the understanding that the author and publisher are not engaged in rendering legal, financial, or other professional advice.
The author and publisher specifically disclaim any liability that is incurred from the use or application of the contents of the book.

Ordering Information: Quantity sales. Special discounts are available on quantity purchases by corporations, associations, and others. Orders by U.S. trade bookstores and wholesalers.

DREAMSTARTERS

www.DreamStartersPublishing.com

KENT A KIESS

Table of Contents

Dedication 4

Introduction 6

Tradition 10

Wants & Fears 18

The Fundamentals of Time 28

Creating More Time and Finding More Time for Yourself 41

The Fundamentals of Health 48

Generational Health 63

Wealth 71

Investing 84

KC-Investments 98

Conclusion 120

Inquiries 123

Books and References 124

Dedication

"This book is dedicated to my son and daughter, Andrew and Kacey. You are the reason behind my actions and the motivation driving my hard work to assist not only myself but others as well. My goal is to demonstrate to you that by pursuing your dreams and putting in the effort, anything is achievable.

I would also like to extend this dedication to my wife, Karen, who is both brilliant and beautiful. Without her, I would be nothing. She consistently provides comfort and solace, never complains or interferes, asks for nothing, and withstands all challenges."

I extend my heartfelt gratitude to my family—Dad, Mom, sister Angie, and brothers Andy and Sean—for their unwavering support.

Thanks to all my coaches, friends, and extended family for being my pillars of strength.

A special appreciation to my past students in Construction for their exceptional dedication.

KENT A KIESS

Deep thanks to our investors who trust us, and, above all, immense gratitude to "The" KC-Investment team for their relentless commitment. Each one of you has played a vital role in our journey, and I am profoundly thankful for the collective effort that has brought us to where we are today.

A heartfelt thank you to everyone who purchased this book! Your support means the world. If you enjoyed it, please spread the word and share the love!

Introduction

Have you ever felt as if time was flying by, money was short, and your health had ghosted you over five years ago? Well, it turns out to be true what they say, "Everything is connected." I spent years trying to understand why I worked so hard but always seemed to come short in these three critical aspects of my life; time, health and wealth.

I finally realized that I was trying to trade my time for money, which is the typical model for never getting wealthy. Instead, it results in there never being enough hours in the day to get done what is needed to make the money to cover the bills, and then, of course, your health ends up covering the difference. You might skip dinner to do a side gig or lose sleep over how you're going to pay the mortgage. Juggling the three crucial aspects of happiness never ends well.

Instead of trying to trade one for the other, there is a way to get those three pesky traits to work together and help each other grow. In other words, having the time to take care of your health allows you to have the energy to create passive income and step off the treadmill of working yourself ragged trying to earn money the old-fashioned way.

I come from a family of construction workers, and I watched as my dad eventually lost his battle trying to hold onto his business after years of self-employment. It doesn't take too many bad economic accidents to make a business tumble. We have all worked on thin margins. Watching that just broke my heart but it also forced me to look hard for a better, smarter way to live.

The secret was finding a way to make money without trading in your valuable time and health. The answer, for me, was investing in real estate. It's a perfect match for us construction people because we already understand so much of how the industry works. I learned how to take all that accumulated knowledge and use it to my advantage. The wonders of passive income through real estate investments created a lifestyle for me that allowed me to become wealthier than I ever imagined while improving my health and having more free time than I could have wished for.

To get there, and I intend to show you exactly how you can do that for yourself, I had to begin with going back and evaluating all of the ways that my learned traditions had supported my scarcity mindset. How they had caused me to believe that hard work is rewarded magically and all that is needed for success is to put your head down and push ahead.

***

This book and the lessons it contains will allow you to see the bigger picture, to understand wealth in a more

BEYOND THE TOOL BELT

comprehensive way, and will teach you how to approach creating the life of your dreams in an efficient, effective way. You will learn about the meaning and consequences of assets and liabilities, the beauty and importance of cash flow, and how to create generational wealth through passive income. In this book, I'm inviting you to explore the principles and insights that will empower you to create generational wealth, while also prioritizing work-life balance and safeguarding both your physical and emotional well-being. We'll take a look at age-old traditions (some healthy, and some not), and how to address our deepest desires and the fears that hold us back. We'll delve into the essentials of health, including how to achieve generational health. And to sum everything up, we'll go over practical lessons about wealth and investment, and what I've learned. Together, we'll embark on a path to a more prosperous and balanced life, driven by these fundamental principles.

      Because, let's be honest, traditional paths to a comfy retirement, such as pensions, are in fact unpredictable, uncontrollable, and simply don't always pan out the way you think they will. Have you seen the stock market lately? To avoid falling into this trap, to prevent that financial insecurity from haunting you when you really just want to be laying out on the beach in the Bahamas with your wife, you have to have a Plan B. Do you have an investment plan in place? Will you be able to have a sustainable passive income stream, so that you can make money while you sleep, or while you're spending your time with your grandkids? If the answer to those questions is currently "no," or if you have yet to even consider those questions, now is the time to make a change and take charge of your future. It starts with looking back at your family traditions and what they taught you about money.

Chapter 1

Tradition

"Continuous improvement in construction is like fine-tuning your car regularly. While there may be upfront costs involved, it ultimately leads to long-term savings by enhancing efficiency and reducing the need for frequent maintenance."

Well, let me tell you about the legendary stubbornness of the Kiess clan. You see, in German, my last name, "Kiess", should be spelled "K-E-I-S-S." But, oh no, that was too mainstream for my ancestors. A long time ago, my great-great-grandpa and his brother had a spat so epic, it probably made soap opera writers envious. They owned so much land, they could've been the original Monopoly men. But instead of making amends, they decided to go their separate ways. And just to be extra petty, my side of the family changed the spelling of our last name. So, voilà, we became the Keiss family; K-I-E-S-S. Take that, brother!

Now, I finally get why I'm so darn stubborn. It's in the genes! Over time, this stubbornness has become as much a part of our DNA as our love for beer and sausages. There are theories that our cravings and food intolerances are based on our ancestors' diets. So, if you ever see me refusing broccoli, you know who to blame.

Tradition is a quirky beast. Most are passed down with the best intentions. Our folks want us to be hardworking, frugal, and practical. Sounds good, right? But here's the kicker: every silver lining has its cloud. Work too hard, and you might just burn out. Save too much, and you might miss out on life's experiences. Be too practical, and you might never learn to think outside the box.

Life's all about balance. If your family traditions are as complicated as mine, sometimes you've got to take that well-meaning advice and sprinkle a little salt on it. Celebrate the good traditions, but always be open to new ideas. Hard work is fab, but so is a Netflix binge occasionally. Saving is smart, but so is investing in that startup your friend keeps yapping about.

Generational traditions can be a mixed bag. Some are gems, while others... not so much. I had to unlearn some of the "work hard and hope for the best" mentality I inherited. But hey, better late than never, right?

BEYOND THE TOOL BELT

Now, don't get me wrong, I've had some great times thanks to my family traditions. Like playing baseball with my mom, who's such a die-hard New York fan, she probably bleeds pinstripes. She was always there, taking foul balls to the face and laughing it off. My dad? He's my hero, my Yoda. And Mom? She's the Wonder Woman of my world. They did their best, and I cherish the lessons they've taught me. But I've also added a few twists of my own. Because that's what traditions are about, taking the old, mixing in the new, and creating something uniquely yours.

***

When I worked in education, I would often listen to my students vent about their personal struggles, be it in regard to their families or finances. I taught in a low-income community and heard time and time again heartbreaking stories of how these students felt held back from the things they wanted to achieve in life due to their circumstances. I wanted to help them so badly, but unfortunately, there was only so much someone in my position could do for them. Although at that time in my life I didn't know what I do now. Today, I would encourage young people to look beyond their life circumstances, and really examine the mindset they've been living with. Often, we don't realize that we've adopted negative thought patterns through no fault of our own, but ultimately, those thought patterns need to change if we want to break free from the generational traditions, specifically the generational curses, we've been afflicted with.

In the grand narrative of career choices, construction often finds itself in the shadows, perceived by many as a last resort or a second-class option. It's a profession often misunderstood, unfairly stigmatized, and marred by misconceptions. From casual stereotypes to societal biases, construction, for far too long, has been burdened with misconceptions that undermine its true potential.

Construction workers are, in fact, the backbone of our society, playing a pivotal role in shaping our physical world. Their contribution to our communities cannot be overstated, as they build the infrastructure we rely on daily, from our homes to our roads, bridges, and schools. The demand for skilled construction workers has reached an all-time high, and it's a trend that shows no sign of slowing down.

A combination of retiring workers and a booming construction industry has led to a significant shortage of skilled labor. As we try to address our aging infrastructure and develop new, sustainable projects, the construction industry is grappling with a shortage of workers that threatens to impede progress.

What surprises a lot of people is that the construction profession often offers better financial rewards than many other career paths. Skilled construction workers can earn competitive wages, with the potential for substantial income growth as they gain experience and expertise. The demand for their skills has driven up salaries, making the construction industry an attractive option for those seeking financial stability and professional growth. This increased compensation reflects the essential role construction workers play in our society and the recognition that they deserve to be rewarded for their hard work, dedication, and the vital infrastructure they create.

The traditional narrative that white-collar jobs offer higher wages and better opportunities is being challenged. Certain blue-collar professions, particularly skilled trades like electricians, plumbers, and welders, may offer more lucrative financial prospects than some white-collar roles. Fortunately, the demand for skilled trades is on the rise, with employment for electricians, plumbers, and welders expected to grow by 8%, 14%, and 3%, respectively, between 2020 and 2030, according to the Bureau of Labor Statistics (BLS).

The fact that there is a shortage of skilled workers has been exacerbated by a cultural emphasis on college degrees, insufficient vocational training programs, and that lingering stigma around blue-collar jobs. Meanwhile, the impact of automation (and artificial intelligence) on white-collar positions is reducing the number of available opportunities and has led to a closing gap between blue-collar and white-collar salaries.

Skilled trade workers also benefit from early-career earnings and the ability to avoid student loan debt.

Plumber or Doctor?

In the grand theater of earning potential, the world often assumes that doctors take center stage, raking in immense wealth while blue-collar workers, such as plumbers, play a supporting role in the financial shadows. But what if I told you that, contrary to the script, plumbers are now giving doctors a run for their money? Let's dissect the astonishing disparity in earning trajectories between plumbers and doctors, showcasing how early income, debt, and career longevity turn the narrative on its head.

Act 1: The Rise of the Plumber

Picture a young plumber. Ok, I'll bite – we can call him Joe the Plumber. Joe's fresh out of vocational training and eager to take on the world. While doctors are busy accruing substantial student loan debt and spending a decade and a half immersed in education and training, our plumber steps into the workforce right away. Today's plumbers are increasingly commanding six-figure incomes, with some of the most skilled among them raking in over $200,000 annually.

BEYOND THE TOOL BELT

Act 2: The Doctor's Dilemma

On the other side of the stage, doctors are grappling with the formidable burden of student loans. Susan is one of those doctors; with the average medical student debt in the United States surpassing $200,000, the first years of a doctor's career are often a financially uphill battle. While the promise of a substantial income beckons for Susan, it's not until the 15th year into her career that she might finally start reaping the rewards of their labor.

The case of "Plumbers vs. Doctors" offers a theatrical twist in the age-old tale of income disparity. Plumbers, who plunge into their careers right from the start, are now emerging as formidable earners in their own right. In contrast, doctors, with their prolonged education and mounting student debt, face a slower climb to financial prosperity.

I encourage you to reevaluate your traditions and keep an open mind as well. If you're reading this, it's likely that you're not entirely satisfied with your own, and that's okay— no one has all the answers, and your traditions have probably done you some good as well. Change can be terrifying, but it's not necessarily a bad thing. Part of being proactive about creating the life you want to live is not turning a blind eye to resources and opportunities that can better your life.

Don't be *that* person, crafting a DIY prison labeled 'inefficiency.' Seriously, ever tried tilting your head and seeing things from a different angle? Or are you just lounging in the comfy chair of 'I'm always right'? I bet there's a brilliant solution out there you've conveniently overlooked. Take a moment, sip your coffee, and wonder: are those age-old traditions secretly plotting against you? Dreaming of a future that's not a dusty replay of yesteryears? Time to shake off the cobwebs. Cherish the tales and wisdom from the ancestors, but maybe, just maybe, sprinkle in your own flair. After all, it's your life's story, not a hand-me-down novel.

Takeaways

- Reflect on your own perceptions of success. Have you been conditioned to believe that a traditional, higher education path is the only route to financial success? Challenge the notion that early financial stability and long-term earning potential must come at the cost of student debt. Reevaluate your career choices in light of these insights.
- What traditions do you think are passed down to you by your family and culture? Which of those would you consider "positive," and which might need to be "adjusted" a bit?

Chapter 2

Wants & Fears

"Generational traditions are like the foundation of a building. Just as a strong foundation supports the entire structure, these traditions provide a solid base for a family or community. Wants are like architectural design - they add style and personality, but without the foundation of needs, the structure lacks stability. So, just as we build a strong foundation before adding the decorative elements to a building, it's important to prioritize our needs, which are like the traditions passed down through generations, before fulfilling our wants."

Generational traditions: the unsolicited life advice we never asked for. Ever heard of the "scarcity versus abundance" mindset? It's like the software update for your brain you keep ignoring. Grew up without a silver spoon, being told to lick your plate clean and hearing the classic "money doesn't grow on trees"? Congrats, you've been primed to live out that budget-friendly adult life.

Now, while it's all very relatable, it doesn't mean it's the gold standard for mental health. Viewing the world through "everything's-on-sale" glasses can lead to some questionable life choices. Sure, our families probably meant well when they passed down these "values." But let's be real, their hand-me-down life strategies might not be our size. If their life story isn't the blockbuster you're aiming for, maybe it's time to rewrite the script.

This whole scarcity vs. abundance drama plays right into our personal soap operas. We all want the dream—chasing passions, being the boss, rolling in dough, and maybe even leaving some for the next generation. So, what's the roadblock? Spoiler alert: sometimes, it's just us being our own worst critic. But why, oh why, do we love this self-sabotage?

It's that pesky fear, courtesy of the scarcity mindset. It's like that annoying voice in the back of your head, always ready with a "told you so" or a "remember when you tripped in public?" every time you spot a shiny opportunity. Trust me, that scarcity mindset? It's the ultimate party pooper.

There is a fascinating study out there conducted by Dr. Jordan B. Peterson involving the role fear plays in life. It entailed motivating one group of rats to run through a maze

BEYOND THE TOOL BELT

with the smell of a cat following behind them, and then motivating another group with the smell of cheese ahead of them, at the end of the maze. Turns out, rats are more inspired to action by their fear of a deadly predator than they are by their favorite treat.

So, how can we apply that study to our own lives? While we may not have tails or be literally on the run from a fanged, hairy beast, many of us are figuratively on the run from our own unique fears. Fear is a powerful, and sometimes very dangerous drug. Sure, fear is great when you have to flee for your life. But often what we are running away from in life is blown out of proportion or is simply irrational.

Change seems to be quite a common fear for many people. But viewing change as a reliably negative thing is a mistake. Change can be for the better—when you make the big decision to switch careers, you may find that it's the greatest thing to ever happen to you, perhaps due to a far higher salary, or simply because you're able do what you love every day (they say if you love what you do you'll never work a day in your life). If you are so terrified of change that your fear becomes your number one motivator to flee from opportunity, your fears are effectively governing your life, and not for the better.

In this sense, let your *wants* in life be your inspiration to action instead. Make sure you're looking in the right direction and embrace the potential for something positive that is waiting for your arrival. Your fears, on the other hand, are likely to chase you to a place you don't want to be.

***

The scarcity mindset that shapes our fears has both short- and long-term consequences. Short-term consequences may go unnoticed in our day-to-day lives, but trust that they are manifesting all around you whether or not you realize it. Every little decision we make has consequences that may influence your future in many unknown ways. Perhaps your fears of embarrassing yourself will talk you out of attending a networking activity, or even more subtly, create reasonable-sounding excuses for you to bail. Maybe your fears of it being "too late" will cause you to refrain from taking up a new hobby you've always wanted to try.

It comes in many shapes and forms. Life is blooming with opportunity everywhere you look—you could have gotten an interview for your dream job at that networking event or discovered that you're in fact quite good at fly fishing. Those little things add up over time, and bleed into long term consequences that may cheat you of these opportunities simply because you let the voice in your head tell you that you weren't worth it.

BEYOND THE TOOL BELT

The long-term consequences? Other than cheating yourself repeatedly of opportunities that could have changed your life for the better, living with a scarcity mindset, living your life in fear, ultimately will always come back to bite you in the ass. Most successful individuals swear by the principles of the law of attraction. It basically provides that "like attracts like," that your thoughts, beliefs, words, and actions all have the magnetic effect of attracting similar things into your life.

For example, if you believe that voice in your head that tells you that you're going to look like a fool in front of a crowd, it's likely that you will work yourself into a frazzled state of little confidence, and thus will in fact end up doing something that makes you look foolish. If you tell yourself that you are not good enough at whatever your profession is, and head to work already thinking you are going to do a terrible job at whatever your boss throws at you that day, your discouragement and lack of confidence in yourself will likely show itself through a sloppy work product.

To live a successful life, we must make it a priority to set ourselves up for success. It may sound cliché, but the first step to success really is believing in yourself and your abilities. Through having a limiting, scarcity mindset, you are riding a completely different wavelength than the one you want to be on—the one where you have the life of your dreams. Know that you are only ever going to be aligned with what is on your wavelength.

So, if you don't like the ride that you're on, you have to shift your mindset and head off in another direction. Even if you do not believe in concepts such as the law of attraction—although if that's the case I strongly encourage you to keep an open mind, and just give those net positive principles a try—it's easy to understand how if you are not in the right state of mind, your decision making is undoubtedly impaired. And when your decision making is impaired, you risk taking actions that are detrimental to your life, whether or not the effects of your actions are apparent to you at that time. It's sort of like waking up on the wrong side of the bed, stubbing your toe on the way to the bathroom, and your day spirals from there.

It might sound dramatic, but it's unfortunately all too common for us to let irrationally negative thoughts stemming from our traditions or low self-esteem, and/or overall insignificant daily occurrences that won't matter five years down the road, to affect us so deeply over the course of time that we have inadvertently gotten ourselves into a pattern, or rather, a vicious cycle, of acting in ways that are not in our best interest.

If you wake up pissed off and let those feelings linger longer than necessary, you'll likely go about your day behaving like a pissed off individual, which often doesn't do you any favors. If you wake up every morning believing that you're unattractive and bad at your job, you probably walk into work incredibly self-conscious, and may be less willing to engage with your colleagues, or afraid to ask for a raise during your annual review despite meeting your sales goals. When the narrative you're telling to and about yourself is *"I'm not worth it,"* the Universe listens and responds accordingly.

But you *are* worth it! Those subconscious fears that are out to get you do *not* have to be your truths—don't trust them! Know that you are free to go after the things you want; in fact, you absolutely should! You will never truly know what good could happen if you never try. It is never too late. It is okay, often even healthy, to break tradition. It doesn't matter what other people think of you. Life is about risk assessment, and risks can often pay off *tremendously*.

I encourage you to read the book, *The Miracle Morning*, by Hal Elrod. The author presents a powerful (and simple) morning routine designed to improve your personal AND professional life. Elrod, after surviving a devastating car accident, was motivated to share this life-changing morning routine that helped him ultimately achieve exceptional success. This book, in short, details the "SAVERS" routine, encompassing practices like meditation, affirmations, visualization, exercise, reading, and journaling, and explains how it can enhance productivity, personal development, and overall well-being, making it a great choice for those seeking a structured approach to self-improvement.

***

KENT A KIESS

Life, just like the economy, is all about the peaks and valleys. There are good times and hard times, ups and downs to this roller coaster that is life. It's just the way it is. And you have to be able to accept that some things in life will ultimately be out of your control, such as whether or not you were born into a wealthy family or to a single-parent household where you're struggling to put food on the table.

When things in life are beyond your control, or hardship unexpectedly falls upon you, it is up to you what you do with that information and how you will respond. It is far more productive to go about life proactively rather than reactively. Our time here on Earth is shorter than we realize—it would be a real shame if we wasted that time dwelling on the bad rather than shaking it off so we can seek out all the good.

Time is a real blessing, like many other simple, yet complex blessings we take for granted every day. The following chapter will introduce you to the fundamentals of time, and you will learn how powerful it can be to learn to manage it rather than letting time manage you. When you are seeking drastic changes in life such as obtaining financial freedom, the greatest first step you can take is to look deep within and ask yourself if you are actively wasting away those blessings and resources that you have been taking for granted all this time.

With time, it is regrettably all too common for people to spend it freely and foolishly on actions that get them nothing and nowhere, rather than learning to have the discipline to spend that time on improving their health, educating themselves, practicing a hobby or skill, or on things that otherwise would bring them joy and general wellbeing. But you are not going to be that person. Instead, you are going to be the kind of person that uses an abundant mindset to effectively go after the things they want with gusto.

"You must be the change you want to see in the world."

Mahatma Gandhi

Takeaways

- *Be who you want to be.* We are all guilty at times of being our own worst enemy. It's okay if you have been that person—you don't have to beat yourself up over the mistakes you have made in the past, and at any moment you can decide to live abundantly in the present by shifting your mindset to the right wavelength. If you're not happy with where you're at, you have to just get up and *move*!
- *Wants & Fears.* Fear is a very powerful motivator in our lives. That fact is not always a bad thing; the issue arises when we let fear guide us rather than being guided by the things we actually want. You have to stay

focused on those desires and not let all that background noise throw you off. Chances are that the fears that are cracking that whip behind you are going to corral you to the wrong pasture.

- *The Catalyst.* Adopting a mindset of abundance will honestly catapult you to success. The right mindset will allow you to effectively better yourself in the areas of life that you are seeking to transform. You will be able to learn and activate the important life lessons in time, health, and wealth that lie herein when you keep an open mind that is ready, willing, and able to absorb such powerful new knowledge.

Chapter 3

The Fundamentals of Time

"Prefabrication is like baking a cake. You can prepare the ingredients in advance and assemble them quickly and efficiently, saving time and money."

Starting Over

    I busted my chops as a teacher. Heck, I even whipped up a construction curriculum for the school, and guess what? It was a hit! Our students were basically the Beyoncés of construction contests—always in the spotlight, always winning. I was the weekend warrior, giving up my summer siestas to make this program shine. I was the school's golden goose, laying golden bricks.

Then, after a glorious twelve-year run, I got this email. My sixth period class? Axed. I had to pinch myself and reread that email, thinking maybe I'd had one too many coffees. Why on earth would they pull this stunt on me?

Here's the kicker: axing a class is like playing Jenga with students' schedules. Some blocks just won't fit anymore. After pouring my heart and soul into this, they decide to throw a wrench in my master plan. I tried reasoning with the powers that be, but it was like talking to a brick wall. So, I did what I always did: nodded, smiled, and played by their rules. Spoiler: it didn't spark joy.

Every time I thought I was on a roll, life, or the economy, or some cosmic joke would trip me up. But hey, I'm an optimist. Every setback? Just life's quirky way of saying, "Let's see you dance out of this one." It's the family motto. But after the umpteenth curveball, I even had to pause.

Post-Christmas break, in a quiet classroom moment, I had an epiphany. "Why am I on this hamster wheel? Working my socks off, getting somewhere, and then—bam! —hitting a wall?" Deep breath. "That's it, I'm tapping out."

But here's the thing: I wasn't really "done." I was just lost. At forty-nine, standing at life's crossroads, I was the poster child for midlife confusion. "What now? Where to? How do I level up from here?"

BEYOND THE TOOL BELT

I read something once that said how at the end of each decade, people do something that they've never done before; how we're always thinking that next decade is a little bit more sand in the hourglass; how we often feel as if time is running out, but we still have so many things on our to-do list. As I was coming up to the end of another decade, I knew that was my cue to reevaluate my life, my beliefs, my future. The main issue for me was the feeling of never being able to get ahead. Although my wife and I had been making decent money, it seemed like we were always running a tight budget and trying to find more money. I wanted to create that money, and it was frustrating that I wasn't where I wanted to be at that age.

If you asked me at age twenty-five where I wanted to be at fifty, I would say that I don't know. So, although I was frustrated, it's not like I *knew* where I wanted to be. But I guess I just wasn't where I *felt* I needed to be. I looked back on my life up until that point and thought, *"Man, I've been working since I was twelve years old."* Sure, I had had some fun here and there, but it just seemed like I had been working for a lifetime, and yet still didn't have the freedom that I longed for, the feeling of not *needing* to go to work for a day.

And so, that's when I started researching, to hopefully find the answer to the same dilemma I had been faced with time and time again.

***

KENT A KIESS

Time is something we all too often take for granted. It passes without us noticing, as we go about our lives, our nine-to-five mundane routines we've become accustomed to. But before we know it, decades have passed, and we're left wondering where all that time went, and what exactly we did with all of it.

I know those feelings all too well. I didn't understand concepts such as "ROI" or "IRR," or even how much I was really making for my time. These things aren't typically taught in school; perhaps you learn how to write checks, manage your money, and watch it disappear, but you're never really taught how to *create* money and wealth in the first place.

A light bulb went off in my head when I was working with my dad. The economy had taken a dump, he ended up having to go work in a factory. I knew he had always planned on me running the family business, and so it was unsurprising when he asked me to do so when I was only fifteen years old, barely old enough to run the concrete trucks out in the middle of nowhere. I was the eldest child, and thus, it was my job to contribute when my family needed money. Although I had to give up playing football and baseball because those sports took place during concrete pouring seasons, I was honestly fine with my situation. I truly enjoyed getting up early in the morning to go to work with my dad; it got me out of school for half a day! I was simply doing what I thought I was supposed to be doing.

BEYOND THE TOOL BELT

However, what I realized was that although I knew how to show up to the plant, drive the truck, pour the concrete, refill the truck with concrete, back and forth—I ultimately didn't know much more than that. Sure, I figured out how to keep books and order materials, but I didn't understand the numbers like I do now; I didn't know how to create *more* money for the company. And to this day, I don't think my dad did either. These were different times, and construction companies back then weren't typically structured the way they are now. He was just doing what everyone else was usually doing, and he was doing a great job in that context.

There were times that the company made really good money, but unfortunately, that money wasn't invested back into the organization; to be sure, construction has its own ups and downs. Eventually, it got to a point where we ended up just selling the company dirt cheap, because it gave us just enough to take care of our family.

That experience was tough, because at that time I thought I was a natural entrepreneur. When I was younger, for instance, I always took odd jobs, such as mowing lawns and selling Christmas cards to the neighbors. But like many folks of my generation, I was taught that in order for me to get something I wanted, I had to work hard for it. The experience of losing the business, despite the hard work of my parents, left us all feeling defeated. They had done their best with what they knew at the time.

KENT A KIESS

I think a lot of people with businesses that don't work out share those feelings. But for me—I wouldn't say that I did much better than my parents had. It's not an excuse, but I just didn't know that other crucial side of the business that I needed to know in order to make the company a success. Could've, should've, would've.

***

Dissatisfied with the way my life was unfolding, I began studying my time, and how I was utilizing it. Gary Keller talks about this in his book, *The One Thing,* where he emphasizes the power of focus and prioritization. Keller, a successful real estate entrepreneur and co-founder of Keller Williams Realty, advocates the simple principle of identifying and concentrating on the single *most important* task at any given moment to achieve results. Keller's key philosophy is based on simplifying (and accelerating) success by cutting through distractions and dedicating your efforts to the most impactful task.

When I assessed this notion from my position as an educator, I realized that I was putting in a tremendous amount of time for my class and students, but I still didn't have any passive income at all. In fact, I had no idea what passive income even meant. Just as important was the realization I came to regarding how much money I was actually making as a teacher (and even when I was making extra money, where was it actually going? The answer to that is likely the government, but I had thought that was the way it was supposed to be, like it was my patriotic duty).

I broke everything down into hours, like all the extra work that I did for the school that I wasn't paid for. Turns out my hourly rate boiled down to around $16 an hour. $16, at forty-nine years old! Forget that. At this turning point in my life, I was overweight, tired, unhealthy—just miserable overall. But I knew that wasn't the kind of guy I was, and that I had to make changes for myself. So, I broke things down even further: I knew if I could get myself to age fifty-five, I could start drawing from my pension. A huge goal of mine at one point was to make it to around age sixty-three, in order to get my full pension as a teacher. Sixty-three didn't sound too bad, but man, those last thirteen years of teaching could be a struggle. So, fifty-five seemed like a good goal.

In a Wall Street Journal article titled "Should You Take a Lump-Sum Pension Payment?" by Glenn Ruffenach, the writer grapples with a decision presented by his former employer: a lump-sum payment of $44,000 or a monthly pension of $423 scheduled to start at age 65. The article sheds light on a growing trend in which more Americans are faced with similar choices as employers offer lump-sum payments to reduce pension liabilities. The decision-making process involves evaluating numerous financial considerations, like the cost of replicating the pension over the potential returns from investing the lump sum. It comes down to personal preferences, risk tolerance, and the impact of inflation on future purchasing power. Not to mention the 'X Factor." Will the pension still be there? (Check out the book, "Who Stole my Pension" by the legendary Robert Kiyosaki for a deep dive on this topic.)

I mention this article as it aligns with the core theme of making informed choices that impact your (and your family's) long-term financial well-being. The author is presented with a dilemma that requires a thorough analysis. At that point in my life, I was too.

I knew I didn't want to get back into construction, because it was very hard work and I was forty-nine and out of shape, and also just because I had been there and done that already. I don't think I could have done it again even if I wanted to, so I had to find another way out of my predicament.

That led me to the discovery of an investment company that basically turnkeys houses and flips them, so that I, as the investor, could purchase it, while the company took care of everything. I dove in and today, I have five single-family residences in Memphis, Tennessee, that I have never even seen, but I make passive income on them each month. It's a beautiful thing.

BEYOND THE TOOL BELT

It's funny that things worked out this way, because when working with my dad, my brother and I would always bounce the idea to him that we should buy a few houses in town, fix them up, and either flip them for a profit or rent them out. But Dad, true to his traditions, said it was too much work, or that tenants don't pay. I know now that these were excuses, but at the time, we just acquiesced, thinking that Dad knows best, and we certainly didn't want to waste our money if that was the case. Of course, hindsight is 20/20.

Several years into our marriage, my wife and I decided to dabble in real estate. We opted for the route of flipping houses, a venture that would not only yield substantial profits but also grant us a clever tax advantage – simply by residing in these properties for a duration exceeding 24 months.

Now, here's where it gets interesting. For the final property that we flipped, I never lifted a hammer. Instead, I donned the hat of a General Contractor, orchestrating the entire operation. We brought in skilled artisans to manifest our vision, and the result was remarkable: the most substantial profit we'd ever pocketed from a house flip. It was quite a lesson in fiscal ingenuity, looking beyond supposed "cost savings" (a la do-it-yourself) to make the most money.

Our real estate escapades weren't just about bricks and mortar; they were a testament to the strategic side of real estate – the importance of leveraging tax benefits and orchestrating a project to our advantage. It goes to show that in the realm of real estate, it's not always about sweat equity; it's about financial aptitude.

It also wasn't about "making a living"; it was about creating wealth, creating a *legacy*. I then came to the understanding that if I wanted to become wealthy, I couldn't be at the properties I bought, spending all my time and energy on being the property manager, doing everything myself—I had to start thinking much bigger. I couldn't wear the hat of project manager, CPA, and toilet-fixer. Mark Cuban once phrased it as, *"It's better to have a quarter of a watermelon than the entire grape."* I was raised that doing things myself was best; but just because those were my generational traditions didn't mean that they were accurate.

Delegating & Outsourcing

When I tried to do everything on my own, I was always exhausted. That was another matter I had to break down into hours. A perfect example is when I was doing all the chemical work on a pool at one of my properties. For a year, I kept track of everything I did for that pool, including the extensive amount of time I put into it. I sure was *pissed* at the end of the year.

When I had our pool redone, I asked the person who did it if he maintained pools. He said yes, so I inquired what he charged. I discovered that he was doing it dirt cheap.

BEYOND THE TOOL BELT

When I compared his numbers with the ones I had collected over the course of a year of my own pool work, I realized that I paid twice as much for doing everything myself!

People often don't understand that so much more goes into taking tasks like this completely upon us. When you intend on taking on a project like this yourself, you still have to have the tools to accomplish it, you still must have the knowledge to complete the project properly, and of course, you still have to have actual the *time* to do it. In contrast, when you hire someone that knows what they're doing, sure, you'll have to spend a little more at first. But if you sat down and really looked at the numbers, you'd realize that it would all be worth it in the long run, when you used all that extra time and energy creating wealth elsewhere. It's the "who," not "how" approach—learning to outsource your weaknesses. It's outsourcing the technically non-revenue producing activities, and instead focusing your time and energy on what *you* do best, whether it's buying and selling houses, or putting the funds together to do so, or otherwise.

The logic is that you calculate your hourly rate (for me, that was $16 an hour), and establish what your "dream" hourly rate is. If your dream hourly rate is, say, $200 an hour, any task paying less than $200 should be outsourced—because your time is more valuable than that. When you break down the numbers, you realize how much of what you've been doing should have been outsourced to begin with.

KENT A KIESS

When you start to outsource tasks like this, it might feel wrong at first—you may feel a bit lazy, or weak. I'm sure many working in construction can relate to those feelings. We're stubborn! I remember when we bought our third house in a really great neighborhood, all the neighbors had gardeners. And of course, I was the one in the neighborhood insistent on doing my own gardening. Why would I hire somebody to do what I could just do myself?

My wiser neighbor would come over, take a good look at the lawn, and say, *"Dude, just hire someone."*
"Nope—my yard's way better looking than yours!" And it was, to be honest.

But on the other hand, I also knew how much time I spent on my yard while my neighbor was instead out golfing, playing tennis, or doing whatever else it is that people with free time enjoy doing.

Personally, I know now that I will never mow the lawn again in my lifetime. I used to take so much pride in doing things myself, now I see how foolish it all was in terms of time and money. When I was in my twenties, I used to say that I never wanted to think that I was too good to mow my own lawn. Those sentiments are certainly admirable qualities for an individual to hold. But it's okay to recognize when you're not the person best suited for the job and that you can instead delegate the task and pivot to something that is a better use of *your* time. Feeling the steadfast need to accomplish anything and everything alone is simply a bad idea, despite the good intentions that may lie behind it.

Takeaways

- *The Fundamentals of Time.* Don't just let time pass you by—examine how you spend your time, and what your time is worth. Determine how much you want your time to be worth. When you figure out that number, use it to guide your decisions as to what tasks should be outsourced to others who can tackle it more efficiently, meaning you'll enjoy the benefit of having that time for yourself to employ in a more productive manner.

Chapter 4

Creating More Time and Finding More Time for Yourself

"Building automation is like a personal assistant for your building. It saves time and money by taking care of the little things, so you can focus on the big picture."

Understanding time is like figuring out the storage capacity of your brain. Think of it as your VIP pass to freedom. Skimp on time and freedom, and guess what? Your relationships and basically everything else that matters will throw a tantrum. Your mojo, your zest, and your eagerness for the next big thing in life start to fizzle out when your brain's bandwidth is maxed out. And let's be real, those are the juicy bits of life.

Now, the art of creating more time? It's like a magic trick I hadn't yet mastered, probably thanks to my "I-know-best" attitude. Raised on the classic "my way or the highway" mantra, I became the poster child for feeling stuck in a rut. Years of nodding along, playing by the rules, and never daring to question if the family playbook was really the gold standard. Guess what? it wasn't.

A lot of people are living with that same mindset of waking in the morning, going to work, completing their assigned tasks, then going home to prepare to do it all over again the next day. But many don't realize that if they just sat down for thirty minutes or so and put together a schedule for the week, they'd find that they'd be so much more productive in the areas of their lives they truly desire to improve.

Look, I was that guy. I'd wake up thinking, "Who needs a plan? I'll just tackle xyz, nail it, and then... oh, look, something shiny!" More often than not, I'd hop to the next task before even finishing the first. It's like being lured by the siren song of that sweet, sweet dopamine hit. Construction folks totally get it. It's in our DNA to be hands-on and dive right in. We're like, *"Why plan when you can hammer?"* But in this gig, there's this itch to keep pushing, only to realize you're on a never-ending treadmill.

But there's a difference between these individuals and those that *do* get things done. The ones that learn to manage their time properly are the ones that become project managers, and even go on to more white-collar jobs.

Most laborers just show up and work their asses off, and that's certainly an admirable quality that deserves respect. But it's important for anyone in these circumstances to recognize the downfalls of that mindset. They likely don't understand that even if all they do is work at that job, they're still going home and attending to other things, perhaps stopping by friends' and family members' homes to assist there. They might not even get home until nine or ten o'clock at night. But they just keep doing the same thing and are often dissatisfied with the consequences. Amazing results could occur if they stop, take a good look at their calendar, and say, *"Okay, I'm going to spend two hours on xyz on Tuesdays and Thursdays, and then I can still get as much done as if I work all week…"*

Scheduling is a critical tool that I love teaching. The basics start with understanding that the classic equation of *"work x time = money"* doesn't always ring true. Personally, it took me a long time to understand scheduling, because truthfully, I'm not the most organized person (or at least, I wasn't). I just didn't know how and would start formulating an organizational system, but then never see it through.

BEYOND THE TOOL BELT

Organization and scheduling are important aspects of teaching—every week, we had to have our lesson plans done, and I was always trying to find a tool that could help me complete my tasks faster. I am the type of person that can have tons of thoughts, but regrettably never write them down. Sometimes when I was teaching, thoughts and ideas would pop into my head, and I'd hear a little voice taking its mental note, *"That's going straight into my folder for next week's lesson!"*

The reality is that I never even had a folder to put those notes in. This lack of organization and structure resulted in me failing to go after whatever great idea I had in my mind; and then, that idea would fizzle out without me even noticing until it was too late. Although some people may feel as if they thrive in this sort of chaos, it unfortunately doesn't work for most people. It certainly wasn't working for me.

They might feel intimidating or uncomfortable at first, but structure and organization are truly our friends, looking to keep us out of trouble, and with our best interests in mind. Moreover, we now have so many tools for structure and organization *in the palm of our hands.* I strongly encourage you to explore different tools and systems to find what works best for you. Perhaps you're a whiteboard person rather than a reminder app person, or maybe you prefer a calendar app over a classic paper calendar hung on the wall above your desk. There's something for everyone, and no one-size-fits-all approach.

Now, my system of organization involves a system that I came across a few years ago called Getting Things Done by David Allen (GTD). I highly recommend getting this book after you are done reading this one. The basics are where any important idea/task/etc. that comes up either goes into my phone or on a Post it notes and placed into my inbox. Then, each week I have a ritual where I go through that inbox and place those ideas/tasks where they belong, meaning, in a category that instructs me what to do with that information and when. This organizational system allows me to get a good sense of what's important and what's not, which keeps me focused and productive when I might otherwise become distracted and discouraged. Often, I'll go through all these notes from the week, and all of a sudden, my inbox is empty before I know it, and I still have half the day left!

This system basically involves outsourcing the tasks and notes to other categories, to give me a good sense of what I need to prioritize. I determine whether something needs to be acted upon immediately, or if it can be done later instead, perhaps with better resources in place that will allow the task to be taken care of more efficiently. The most important tasks are sorted into other files based on whether they can be completed immediately or if they're a project that needs other people involved. The goal is to eventually have

BEYOND THE TOOL BELT

that task make it to a final point, where it is completely done and crossed off whatever to-do list you call a system like this.

You can experiment with how to design your to-do list, or whatever other organizational system you decide to employ, but the key is understanding whether or not a task is actionable and categorizing it accordingly. This helps tremendously with prioritizing and getting a sense of what's important during your day and allows you to discover what the best use of your time is. Ultimately, in order to put the fundamentals of time into practice, to create more time, to learn to schedule, we must master the art of consistently prioritizing every wish, dream, task and idea.

Obviously, our minds all work differently, and what specifically works for me may not work as well for someone else. However, it's my duty as a teacher and coach to share what has helped me. Perhaps after reading about my system, you'll realize that a similar flowchart happens in your mind all the time.

I wish I had learned to systemize my time many years ago. A lot of people have plenty of free time, and yet waste it on non-productive activities. My goal now is to do the complete opposite: when I do have some free time, I want to use all the time I've created for myself to the absolute fullest. You'll find that doing the same will allow you to be productive, with a great momentum to catapult you further into greatness.

Takeaways

Structure. Creating structure and organizational systems for yourself is life changing in that it allows you to schedule yourself more efficiently, which in turn leads to you creating more time for yourself. Once you have successfully carved out that sacred time, the possibilities of what you can do with it are truly limitless.

Maybe you'll use those extra hours on Thursday nights to pursue an artistic passion, take up a new language, take a college course on a subject you genuinely want to learn more about or work on your "side hustle" (that may very well turn into a life changing thing). Whatever your goal may be, if you don't currently have such structure, it can never hurt to try something new. You may very well find that a kooky, colorful "Post Its" system, or a particular app, or an elegant journal and pen, is the thing that changes your life, and allows you to live up to your full potential in every area of your life.

"The key is over time. Success is built sequentially. It's one thing at a time."

Gary Keller

Chapter 5

The Fundamentals of Health

"Safety is the foundation of any construction project, just like good health is the foundation of a happy life."

For those of us who practically have "workaholic" as our middle name, self-care isn't exactly on the daily menu. We thrive on the thrill of the grind, being the go-to person, and basking in the glow of everyone's "oohs" and "aahs." But here's the kicker: playing superhero 24/7? Yeah, it comes with a price tag.

The secret sauce to not burning out? Learning to say "no." And I get it, those with a killer work ethic often double as serial people pleasers. But thinking you're the Energizer

Bunny can be a trap. Before you know it, you're the one running on fumes after weeks of non-stop hustle. And it's not just about the body. Trying to be the life of the party when you're running on empty? It's a mental and emotional buzzkill. Remember, your brain needs some TLC too.

The Wake-Up Call

While wake up calls in life undoubtedly serve a purpose and end up doing us a lot of good, they are something that no one really wants to experience. It's a slap in the face, a rude awakening that all is not well, that something needs to change. This is naturally a stressful experience, but if you want to prevent those wake-up calls from occurring in the first place, you must learn the lessons they're screaming at you.

For me, that wake-up call came one day after getting off a call with my school's administrator. It was a very stressful time in my life. I was feeling so dissatisfied and frustrated by my career and frustrated by how I had gotten to that point after working so hard my whole life trying to do things the "right" way. When I hung up from that call, I started having trouble breathing. I had never had any issues like that before—I was actually concerned that I was having a heart attack. Of course, back then I was walking around with the attitude I had been raised to abide by—deal with it, shake it off, fight it off.

BEYOND THE TOOL BELT

Turns out I was having my first real anxiety attack, but that experience triggered alarming thoughts along the lines of, *"Am I seriously going to let my students watch me have a heart attack?"*

There was a similar health incident the summer prior to that where I ended up getting Bell's Palsy. Right after school let out for the summer, I started having a strange feeling in my mouth. I woke up the next morning expecting another mundane day, but when I looked in the mirror while getting ready for work, I was horrified to see that my whole face had somehow shifted. *"Did I just have a stroke?"* Thankfully not, but it was still something I never anticipated would happen to me.

My body had become so run down over time as a result of living an unhealthy lifestyle filled with stress and running myself into the ground over things that weren't doing me any favors in life. It happens to many individuals, even the most successful of individuals, such as dedicated, hardworking straight-A students and athletes. When I coached basketball, the coaches would all go so hard during the season that after it was over, we would all get sick for a week or so. After that jarring experience and after the call with the school administrator, I realized just how hard that year had been on me, Between fighting for the curriculum I believed in, struggling with my weight, and feeling self-conscious about the way people reacted to me wanting to change up my inner circle, it all just came crashing down on me and reminded me that I am not, in fact, invincible. It hit me hard that I was not getting any younger, and my health was no longer something I could just shove aside for another day.

That anxiety attack, Bell's Palsy, the sickness I felt after a season of coaching, were all symptoms of a lifestyle I needed to either fix or escape from entirely. I regret waiting for that final wake-up call to make better decisions about my health. When your body is trying to tell you something, you should listen, or it will just start to yell louder until it's heard! It reminds me of the guy who had back spasms when he was out playing golf only to discover that he was minutes away from a heart attack. His body threw a back spasm in there to stop him from golfing and saved his life.

Be vigilant about how you're feeling, because chances are if something feels off, your instinct is correct. Really take a step back and check in on yourself. If you simply feel *bad,* day in and day out, recognize that is not normal.

We tend to take better care of our cars than our bodies. Who among us would simply put a piece of tape over the oil indicator on our car when it's flashing red and keep driving? That's exactly what we're doing when we take a pill to cover up a symptom. Luckily that golfer hadn't taken a muscle relaxant before playing golf.

***

BEYOND THE TOOL BELT

There is much more to health than seeking out a doctor when we're too sick to function, and popping pills to put a bandage on bothersome symptoms so that we can pretend the underlying issues aren't there. Our health is ultimately the most important thing we have in life, and maintaining it is key to accomplishing anything else you want in life.

The first step is to fix our attitude regarding health and realize that treating it as an afterthought is foolish. To transform our lives for the better, we must take accountability for our health, and realize that the time to be responsible for it was yesterday.

The Holistic Approach

Listen up: Your body isn't some hand-me-down gadget you can just reboot when it glitches. Owning your health is like admitting you've got the remote control. Want to strut your stuff feeling like a million bucks daily? Then don't trudge around like you've been hit by a discount shopping cart. Newsflash: You can't ace life's tests when you're feeling like last season's leftovers. Play fast and loose with your health, and it'll come back, haunting you like that embarrassing comedy club hypnotist video from the year '05. Think of preventive care as your body's platinum membership. And let's be real, maybe you've been your own worst enemy, with those midnight snack raids and "just one more episode" promises. Don't wait till your body sends you a "we need to talk" memo.

Jumping into your health's deep end isn't like trying the latest fad diet because everyone's doing it. It's more like a project that needs some solid research. But hey, don't sweat it—you can take baby steps. Every tidbit of health wisdom you gather? That's a gold star. And no, you don't need to morph into a kale-loving, marathon-running, meditation guru overnight. Start with the basics. Maybe it's rethinking that sugar addiction or finding your chill after life threw you a curveball. Every move matters. Kick off your health glow-up, and soon you'll be living your best, brag-worthy life.

Many concepts involved in a holistic approach to health are based in Eastern medicine and traditions from thousands of years ago, such as acupuncture (trust me, acupuncture is life-changing for managing so many different symptoms). Turns out, back in those days they experienced many of the same health issues we struggle with today. They figured out effective methods for addressing those issues, but regrettably, those things somehow got lost, or the healthy traditions of those cultures unfortunately never made their way over to us.

So, I took a detour into the world of holistic health when I realized my waistline was, well, expanding. My snoring had reached concert-level decibels, to the point where my wife considered noise-canceling headphones or just fleeing the scene. I wasn't about to get hooked on some Darth

BEYOND THE TOOL BELT

Vaderesque machine. Enter holistic doc. A bit of blood work, and bam! Thyroid issues. Then came the sensitivity test, which is basically your body's Yelp review. And guess what? My body gave gluten a one-star rating. And what's packed with gluten? Only the best things in life—bread and beer! The betrayal!

    The sensitivity test was great because it showed the equation of what my body needed to get it feeling how I wanted to feel. We were able to put together an action plan for my needs, including drinking more water, having a protein shake every morning on my way to work, and just eating better in general. I became a master in gluten-free cooking, because that's what I had to do to reach my health goals. When I started giving a shit about what I was fueling my body with, I started feeling so much better. I had more energy; now, at nine o'clock at night I'm ready to go to bed, and when I wake up in the morning, I'm feeling great, ready to tackle whatever the day has in store for me with confidence that my body will come through for me.

***

    I firmly believe that a holistic approach to anything in life is the better path to travel. Regarding our health, it's not enough to just be reactive, only seeing a doctor in the event of an emergency, eating poorly until our stomachs protest, running around on only a few hours of sleep, drinking to the point of being hungover the next day. It's like pulling out the batteries when your smoke detector starts going off and laying back down on the burning mattress!

The first step to developing a more holistic approach to health is to step back and look at your body the way you'd look at the deck of an old house. Someone might have slapped a new paint job on it, but there are still rotted planks in there waiting for someone to trust them not to give way. What is your body's back porch trying to tell you?

We get one body, folks. It's not a lease with an option to upgrade. A savvy person schedules that annual peek under the hood (aka a physical); they see a dentist without being bribed with a lollipop; they catch those Z's; they eat balanced meals, not just daily donut binges; and they break a sweat, not just for the 'gram, but to keep things running smoothly.

Once you've mastered the art of time, you'll be all about that proactive life. Heck, it might even become your second nature. Sure, being proactive sounds like a chore, but trust me, it's a time-saver. It's like giving your stuff some TLC rather than waiting for it to fall apart. Because sometimes, there's no duct tape solution.

Some things just gotta come first, and health is top of the list. It's like the airplane oxygen mask rule, but for life. It's not rocket science, but we often forget. Before playing superhero for others, make sure you're not on the verge of a meltdown. Because dreams built on shaky health? That's a house of cards waiting to tumble.

***

So, what else goes into a holistic approach to one's health? Well, it certainly takes an open mind, especially for those who don't think about health beyond taking a pill when they're in pain.

Health really starts in the mind, because the mind inspires the body to action, including the act of self-care. Even if you think your mental health is solid, it's important to check in on your emotions and state of mind. Stress, despite being such a common, shared experience across many cultures, is often underestimated. It takes a toll on both the body and mind. You may not realize it creeping up on you, but it can manifest when you least expect it: an outburst at a loved one after a long day at work, hair loss, teeth grinding and jaw tension, difficulty making decisions, binge eating—the list goes on and on.

Mental health, of course benefitted by modern medicine, is often still a tricky thing to treat and maintain. This is where a holistic approach really shines—there are plenty of proactive, positive, and healthy actions we can take to maintain a healthier and happier mind. Majorly beneficial acts include meditating, exercising, and reading, among other things.

Meditation. I know, who has time for that nonsense? But I bet you are already doing meditation and don't even realize it. It can be as simple as sitting in the backyard and enjoying the view. Meditation is all about being able to clear your mind of whatever's gunking it up and simply *being*. I can remember driving in rush-hour traffic and realizing that I was holding my breath! Talk about stress. I learned to look beyond the traffic, admire the mountains in the distance, and take a few deep breaths.

Although meditation, specifically the part that includes clearing your mind, can sound impossible, it's easy to get started—all you have to do is focus on your steady breathing. There are even apps that can help guide your breathing exercises if you need the extra structure and support. You might have even forgotten how good steady breathing feels because you take your breath for granted! From there, you can work your way up to clearing your mind and letting thoughts drift on by for the time being. And after that, there's so many heights your meditation practices can reach.

Check online for a wide variety of free guided meditations, and see which ones feel good to you. If it feels good, then that means you're on the right track. Managing my stress levels in this way has been life changing. I'm now a more relaxed individual even when not meditating. And if I feel myself getting worked up, I go through my deep breathing exercises and---Voila! I'm in my favorite place by the ocean. That practice brings me back down to Earth when otherwise I might feel my blood boiling.

This "Zen" mentality moved me so deeply that I started bringing it to the players I coached. Some parents got upset by it, because they thought we were wasting our time on exercises such as deep breathing. I used to be the guy out there on the bench screaming. But we can learn a lot from individuals such as Phil Jackson, who instead sat back relaxing, taking those deep breaths, keeping his emotions in check, and got excellent results in return. When I followed his example, when I became more intentional about my state of mind and brought that to my own players, I realized that that was one of my best seasons of coaching. I think I got more out of those players than anyone else would have! At the end of the day, getting yourself worked up so easily, and not understanding how to come back from it, will only hold you back in life.

Exercise. Exercise is another health building block. You don't have to hate exercise, I promise! Even if you're already in great shape, don't have a particular aesthetic goal in mind, or just know that you're never going to be the workout "type," it's crucial just to keep it moving. Your body wants to stretch and use its muscles, not let them sit idly all the time and wither away. If you're starting from zero or have no idea where to even begin, try just going for a walk around the block. See the sights, hear the sound, smell the roses, and simply enjoy being a person in the world, out and about. Then, extend your walks, and try to make them a regular part of your routine. Because you got the initial little bit of momentum, you may then go on to decide to take up running, strength training, or pickleball. Rather than viewing exercise as a chore or even a punishment, treat it as an act of self-care, a luxury, and a privilege. It's for both you and future you, and future you will certainly thank you when it's able to fulfill all the crazy things on your bucket list. In sum, exercise is a critical component of preventative health care, and it adds both quality and quantity to your years, trust me.

Reading. I have a feeling that despite not always saying it out loud, many of us have a negative relationship with reading because of our experiences in school. Some are lucky, going to excellent schools that instill the value of reading in our impressionable minds, and go above and beyond to foster a love of it. But maybe you're one of those that didn't have an influential teacher or even a parent that made it a point to instill that joy in you. That's okay—not all of us have been moved by a great book that sparked a love for reading (yet).

Or maybe, your relationship with reading is on the rocks because you studied so hard that you forgot reading was for leisure, fun, and self-growth as well as for schooling.

BEYOND THE TOOL BELT

Either way, when we hold onto these negative feelings, we miss out on something that can be so enjoyable if we just give it a chance. If you are considering giving it a second chance, know that there's a world of wonder out there for you to rediscover.

Why make reading a part of a holistic healthcare approach? It's simply a healthy, and unquestionably positive pastime that can only better your life. It'll help keep your mind sharp well into old age. Maybe you become engrossed in an epic series that you won't even imagine how you could have missed out on.

Maybe you learn something incredibly interesting that you'll want to further explore, such as ergodic fiction, or Norse mythology. Or maybe you'll pick up an inspirational guidebook such as this one and discover ideas you can use to transform your life *(nudge)*. Whatever this hobby blesses you with, you'll have received some net benefit from your time, that was better spent than if you had spent several hours at a bar for the third time this week, "doom scrolling" on Twitter, arguing with your second cousin on Facebook or eating potato chips on the couch watching reruns of that show you've seen every episode of many times over. It's okay to switch it up sometimes!

Takeaways

- *The Fundamentals of Health.* Listen to your body—often, it sends out warning signals when something is wrong. Don't have the old school "suck it up" attitude when you don't feel right. Recognize that you may very well be causing your own sickness through an unhealthy lifestyle, and that changes must be made before even further damage can be done. *You are not invincible.* None of us are young or old. Your health, at every age, but even more so once you've reached middle age, should *always* be your number one priority in life—you can't just pay attention to it when it's convenient for you, or when you're knocked on your ass with no other option but to address what's ailing you. Before you can transform any other area of your life, you must have a properly functioning body.
- *Try the holistic approach to health.* The best thing you can do to improve your health is to shift your mindset to that of a proactive, rather than reactive approach. Preventative health care can save you so much trouble in the long run, and as time goes on, you'll be incredibly grateful for all the positive steps you took to maintain the only body you're going to get in this life. Take some time to educate yourself further on things like eastern medicine and talk to your doctor about

BEYOND THE TOOL BELT

whether some of those practices could benefit you. Consider getting a second opinion from a doctor with a different philosophy from the one you're used to. Chances are, you'll hear praise from multiple professionals for basic healthy practices such as meditation, exercise, and reading. Feeling good is about both your physical and mental health—make it a point to attend to numerous different components of your health and find that sense of balance that is the foundation for living your best life.

Chapter 6

Generational Health

"Building a green building is like investing in your future health. It may cost more now, but it pays off in the long run."

Crafting generational health isn't about a crash course in kale smoothies. Think marathon, not sprint. Or better yet, the tortoise and the hare. Spoiler: You're the tortoise. No need to go full throttle or turn every workout into a near-death experience. It's all about that steady groove. The real buzzkill? Those who set a 60-day "new me" challenge, then revert to couch potato mode faster than you can say "Netflix binge." Rinse and repeat.

BEYOND THE TOOL BELT

Your body's like a finicky car. Feed it junk, and it'll sputter and stall. Expecting peak performance on a diet of donuts and energy drinks? Good luck with that. If you're not setting yourself up for success, don't expect a victory lap. When you're in top form, you're basically unstoppable.

Here's the silver lining: good habits are clingy. Once they latch on, they're hard to shake off. Start small, think big, and aim for habits that stick around longer than your latest diet fad. Each tweak you make today could add years to your life's scoreboard.

Fast forward, and you'll be the envy of those still deciphering their body's Morse code. Ever notice how some older folks measure health by the "I woke up, so it's a good day" standard? But is that the bar we're setting? Just... existing? Nah. For me, generational health is about keeping up with my kids without needing an oxygen tank. Shift your focus, give your body the royal treatment, and live a life that's more "epic adventure" and less "meh."

Ultimately, it all ties into using your valuable *time* wisely. For example, by reading this, you're already on the right track. I hope that a nugget of information in these pages will give you the momentum to find a moment of calm and steady breathing today, and maybe you'll even feel inspired enough to go for a walk around the block.

Creating Healthier Habits

It's easy to talk about all that we should do for health, but it's not always easy to implement these changes. You may face external obstacles such as financial resources or disability, or even just the internal block of the lack of motivation to make change. Know that those things are okay, and you don't have to be left out of the blessing that is good health—health is for everyone, and you can make it work for you if you just get a little creative.

I'm a firm believer that momentum is key, and that the way to get started is by changing your habits. Start with your morning. What is the first thing you do when you wake up? If you reach for the phone to check emails or look at the lovely world news, that's a no-brainer of a place to begin. It could be as simple as taking a moment to be grateful for the day, your life, your family. Any quick positive thoughts! If you do this enough days in a row, it starts to happen automatically, that's all habits are, after all. Try it for a month and see what changes!

I always say that we are either taking a step towards better health with our actions, or a step away. It's our choice. Life is not static. So, which way are you walking? Are you stepping closer to a heart attack, gaining a few pounds every year? Or are you heading towards toning those muscles and shoring up that sagging back porch of yours?

BEYOND THE TOOL BELT

If you are heading in the wrong direction, all it takes is one small step at a time the other way.

"Success is a journey, not a destination. The doing is often more important than the outcome."

Arthur Ashe

It's a bit like "making your money work for you,"—when you build a better routine, eventually good health won't even feel like that much of an effort; you'll feel so good and enjoy it so much that you'll have forgotten you had to try at all.

To develop that great routine, look at your habits, and which of them aren't working for you. If you're only getting five hours of sleep at night, feel like shit every morning, and go on to struggle focusing on work, then a habit of going to bed at three in the morning and fighting with the alarm clock every day is not going to be a habit that works for you. If your breakfast consists of a cup of coffee and a doughnut, that habit might be a good place to start.

Of course, breaking a bad habit is far easier said than done. But I think it can help to have a positive, forward-looking outlook on making difficult changes in your life. Rather than see it as having to give up your morning doughnut, look forward to the delicious healthy breakfasts you'll have instead.

KENT A KIESS

A protein shake? Or just add some fruits and veggies to go along with some scrambled eggs?

***

Positive habits begin in the morning, from the second you open your eyes. When you start your day off on the wrong foot, it's very easy for your day, and your mood, to spiral from there. Take the preventative approach by working to avoid that spiral and the consequences it'll result in. You don't have to jump out of bed with joy, if that's not your thing but, like I mentioned, gratitude is always going to set your mind on the right track, after that, the day is yours to design. Many take comfort in a hot cup of coffee first thing while others will put on a podcast to motivate them. The important thing is to get you in the right state of mind to achieve everything you want to achieve that day.

Ultimately, all of our goals for what we want to get out of our day, and all of our needs to achieve those goals, will be different. Only you truly know what's best for you. But I would encourage anyone to make it a point to start your day off right, and actively avoid things you already know aren't doing you any favors. That's just a waste of time, and *we won't let time be the dictator of the quality of our lives.* Those two shifts in your routine alone have immense power. You don't have to feel obligated to do more than the bare minimum if you don't want to, but it's far more likely that that momentum will inspire you to become the architect of your days, and you'll seek out opportunities to improve numerous other habits.

You might decide to add in a morning meditation, or a thirty-minute workout before you shower, or read a chapter in whatever book you're currently engrossed in. You might start listening to a motivational speaker or begin practicing a new language on your drive to work. *Find* and *create* that time for yourself, make it work for you, and let it improve your health, wealth, and overall quality of life in the process.

If you grew up like me, chances are a lot of these ideas are foreign to you. To us, they seem non-traditional, but to others, it is their tradition. We don't have to take it personally, the realization that our traditions are not necessarily healthy ones. It's not a right versus wrong thing; our traditions are all just different.

You don't have to be trapped within that neat box if you don't want to be. If there's something in another's tradition that inspires you, go for it, unapologetically. Mix and match your generational traditions with others and create the customized life you want for yourself. No one can do that but you. That is how generational traditions are created in the first place. Be the rebel and replace negative actions and thought patterns with ones that serve you well. You deserve it!

***

KENT A KIESS

Chances are you're reading this book not for this "hippy-dippy shit", but rather for tips on how to transform your life financially. I get it, I really do. I was the same way. But time, health, and wealth are tightly woven together, and there's nothing we can do to change that. You won't be able to create more wealth unless you master the lessons on time and health. And more importantly, money means nothing if you're in poor mental or physical health and don't make time to be with your loved ones. Those are the things that really matter in life, and deep down we all know it. The wealth and all the good that comes of it are ultimately extras, optional parts that we don't really need to be happy.

But if the opportunity to create generational wealth presents itself, there's no reason for us to ignore it. When you understand how to create the life you want with regard to time and health, other things will start falling into place. And when you're living in that abundant state of mind, good will start coming your way. So go on reading and discover how you can reap the benefits of your new outlook on life and use them to design your life with all the fine details.

Takeaways

- *The Power of Positive Habits.* A key part into sparking change that will create generational health is creating healthier habits in order to live a sustainable healthy lifestyle. Look beyond your short-term goals, such as the five pounds you want to drop before your sister's wedding, and instead focus on your overall health and how you can go about transforming that aspect of your life for good. As with most things in life, it will take some maintenance on your part; but trust that learning to respect your body and truly value your health is something that you will treasure over time.

Chapter 7

Wealth

"A carpenter's saw is like a tool for building generational wealth. Just as a saw is used to cut lumber into pieces that can be assembled into a structure, building generational wealth requires careful planning and investment to create a solid financial foundation that can be passed down to future generations. A carpenter's saw is an essential tool for constructing a building, and financial tools like investments, savings, and estate planning are essential for building generational wealth."

So, let's recap our little chat. Generational traditions? Sometimes they're more like outdated software. Just had an "Oops, I've been doing it all wrong" moment? Welcome to the club! The real game-changer? What do you do next.

BEYOND THE TOOL BELT

Ever caught yourself giving the stink-eye to those swanky "rich" folks, sipping their overpriced lattes? It's super tempting to host a "Why not me?" pity party, especially when you've been grinding away, and your bank account still looks like a student's.

Growing up, my money-making theories were simple: inherit a fortune, marry someone who did, or pray for that lottery win. But let's be real: sulking in the corner because you didn't make this year's billionaire list? Not the best strategy. Instead of drowning in envy, how about we play detective and learn from the big shots? (And hey, if you're curious, just ask. I'm practically an open book.)

Here's the cold, hard truth: Most of us are wandering in the financial wilderness, clueless about building that golden empire. But fear not! Every mogul starts somewhere. This chapter is your treasure map. We'll dive into the nitty-gritty, from mastering budgeting to unlocking the secrets of financial freedom. Ready to join the ranks of the financial-savvy? Let's roll up those sleeves and dive in!

The Fundamentals of Wealth

The most important skill you can develop to improve your financial health is learning to manage your money properly. It's easy to spend money, but it can be hard to learn how to be truly responsible with it.

As Robert Kiyosaki so clearly put it in the great classic, *Rich Dad, Poor Dad*:

> *"An asset puts money in my pocket. A liability takes money out of my pocket."*

So, by this definition, not all debt (a liability) is bad, only debt that doesn't make you money. If you buy a condo on the beach and it sits vacant when you're not there, that is not an asset, even though many count real estate as one. Of course, if you are renting it out and earning the mortgage and then some, it most certainly is. I like to say that a person who buys a car or a house on credit doesn't *own* that house or car, they *owe* it. Poor suckers. Let's dive in and tell the truth about debt.

Good vs. Bad Debt

A few years back, a friend of mine complained to me that she wasn't making enough money. When I suggested that her most imminent issue was all the bad debt that she had weighing her down, she was confused as to how some debt could be bad while other debt could be good. I pointed out that in her instance, the boat she had sitting outside was one of the problems.

Anything that floats or flies, you don't want to have debt on. That also goes for fancy cars, unproductive credit card debt, and even debt on the house you're living in. I remember this well in my own history; Money I spent in my younger years meant I was driving around a brand-new red Camaro Iroc Z with T-tops (ok, I know that 'ages' me!), when I could have been purchasing a rental property for passive income.

    Bringing this up, my friend responded that she needed those things, that they were "essential and necessary." When I asked her why she needed her car, she answered that she needed transportation to get to work. Well, that was obvious—but did she really need a brand-new car, or would it be financially wiser to hop on Facebook Marketplace and find a vehicle for a couple thousand dollars that could get her safely from Point A to Point B? After all, she only needed to travel three quarters of a mile to work; it might very well be financially wiser to take an Uber or Lyft, or perhaps even ride her bike.

    On the other hand, equity is often erroneously equated with good debt. But for a debt to pass as "good," it's got to provide you with *cash flow* every month. The house you own and live in, therefore, is technically not an asset, but rather a liability, because it's not making you money. Ten years down the road, the property you bought may be worth more, but at the end of that thirty-year mortgage, you'll usually have paid double for it. And while your house might be worth twice as much at that point, you'll still have effectively made zero.

KENT A KIESS

The average person likely has no idea how much money they spend on the home they own, such as property taxes, homeowners' association fees, expenditures made on improving the property, and more. I didn't realize these things initially either! I eventually examined my own budget that I had developed, including what I had budgeted for my house, and came to the conclusion that renting was cheaper than owning. In fact, it wasn't even close to how much cheaper it was to rent as compared to when we owned our home—we probably saved a good thousand dollars a month! If you're interested in a financial worksheet statement don't hesitate to email me or pull one off the web.

***

Determined to help my friend get back to a financially healthy place, we started breaking down her assets and liabilities in an Excel spreadsheet. She revealed that she was only making minimum payments on her debts each month. This is one of the worst things you can do—with the added interest, it could take you decades to pay that debt off! This fact discouraged her, and she explained that she wasn't making enough each month to make more than the minimum payment.

So, we set up an action plan. Her husband ended up getting rid of his truck, and she ended up selling her car. With those weights lifted, the next step was to figure out how she could make more money. Ultimately, she needed a raise and to use her entrepreneurial skills to create more money, some passive income, beyond her W-2. This would allow her to bring down her taxes, increase her cash flow, and thus bring more money into her budget.

  If you come from a construction background like me, you likely are surrounded by the culture of having big trucks, boats, homes, etcetera. Many of us, across various backgrounds and industries, are further tempted by lavishly spending on things such as fancy dinners, new shoes, jewelry, or other "toys." If these things aren't making you any money and are digging your financial hole even deeper in the process, then you cannot afford them. That day will likely come when you can, but you can't ever get to that place if you don't learn how to manage the money you *do* have. And if you work on your passive income, you could easily accomplish those goals within ten years or so.

  Your income taxes are another area to take a good look at to see if there's room for improvement. The system is set up to reward entities rather than people, especially ones that have a large W-2. If you work as an independent contractor, have a "side hustle," or run a business, it could be helpful to set up an LLC or some other formal business entity to take advantage of tax incentives that you can use to lower that W-2 taxable income.

When you have a chance, check out Tax Free Wealth by Tom Wheelwright. It's a comprehensive guide to understanding the intricacies of tax laws and strategies for minimizing tax liabilities, while legally reducing the amount of income paid to the government. Wheelwright, by the way, is a certified public accountant and wealth strategist. He draws on his extensive expertise to demystify the tax code and provides practical advice on leveraging tax incentives and deductions to build and preserve wealth.

A great deal of the expenses you incur to do your job, such as construction materials, tools, work boots, your vehicle, gas, your phone, your Internet, a work computer, and numerous other things, can be written off on your taxes with this arrangement. Your business can work for you as well! Do your due diligence and take the time to figure out what will get you more for your work and decrease the amount of taxes you pay. Start by creating a team; your CPA, bookkeeper, holistic doctor, chiropractor, etc. Trust me on that one. And read Wheelwright's book!

***

It's often said that cash is king. But I don't believe in that, I believe that *cash flow* is king. Cash flow is the key to creating wealth, and ultimately, financial freedom. It takes a little work (well, sometimes a lot), but once you get that snowball rolling, you can use your cash flow to create more wealth, perhaps by growing your own company. To make these transformations in your financial life (which will positively affect other areas of your life, such as your time and health), you have to put your money to work.

My recommendations? Get some clarity as to your financial stance by breaking down your assets and liabilities. Be honest with yourself as to what you can and can't afford. If your bad debts are keeping you from thriving, rid yourself of them if possible. You may even need to sell everything that you're in debt to. You are owing less and owning more with each sale.

Be patient in regard to the material things and lavish experiences that you may desire. When you've truly earned them, you'll enjoy them more, because they won't come with the added guilt, buyer's remorse, and/or financial burdens. Further, take a good look at the home you live in and what it costs you. Do the math, and if it's going to save you money every month, strongly consider renting instead of owning, the money you'll save can be put to better use, such as allowing you to make more than those minimum payments you've been chained to. And once you get your liabilities in check, you can move on to creating a healthier budget so that you don't make the same mistakes that have been keeping you on that hamster wheel.

Feel free to reach out to our website: www.kc-investments.com or email: kent@beyondthetoolbelt.com

Budgeting

Excel spreadsheets are a great way to organize your finances in a way you can easily visualize and understand. You don't have to be an accountant or a tech guru, just open the software and start inputting your monthly net income and expenses so you can see where your money is at. Now go back and look at the numbers, they don't lie. If you determine that you're in the negative, you've probably been in the negative for years, likely racking up unproductive credit card debt. The time to start working that out is now.

The Magic Number

Most people are unfortunately living paycheck to paycheck. Sometimes, it's really not about the amount of money they make, but rather about how much of it they spend. Many people enjoy a great income but make the mistake of living well above their means, meaning that at the end of the month, all that money they made is effectively gone.

The "magic number" is different for us all—it's your personal freedom number, referring to the amount of money that you need to "break free" of living paycheck to paycheck, and the amount of money that you need to achieve your personal goals. What's most important is first getting yourself back to a healthy financial stance.

Once you've done that, and created a healthy budget, take the time to consider how much money you really *need* to achieve your reasonable, realistic goals. Your magic number does not necessarily have to be one that allows you a Lamborghini and a ten thousand square foot home. But if you reach your magic number, trust that you're eventually going to get that dream home.

Sure, a W-2 provided me the ease and predictability of having money come in and taxes taken out, but I hated feeling that, despite not spending lavishly, having huge expenses, or racking up debt, I could still never really get ahead. It took me a while, but eventually I came to the realization that for me to achieve my goal of breaking free of my W-2, I needed to obtain a cash flow of $6,500 a month.

The knowledge of my magic number drove me to look into using debt productively (good debt), which led me to begin investing in single-family residences in Memphis so that I could achieve the cash flow I aimed for.

Trust me, it's not as difficult as you might think to become financially free! Determining your magic number is important because it helps you break everything down to a more manageable level, thus guiding you toward your goals in a way that isn't as overwhelming. When you break down your action plan into more manageable goals and milestones, it'll allow you the momentum you need to build more wealth.

You'll gain confidence in knowing that all you need to achieve your goal is, say, three single-family investment properties, or to be a partner on two multifamily investment deals, for example. Maybe you only need to achieve an income of $3,000 a month, or at least enough to make twice the minimum payment on that pesky store credit card you got on a whim three Christmases ago.

Whatever your goals and needs might be, understanding where you're at and where you want to be is the first step in determining what needs to be done. And the moment your inputs passively exceed your outputs, you'll be free forever.

***

When it comes to financial hesitancy and stubbornness, I often think of two brothers who owned a construction business together that I used to work for. They would always argue about money, one always wanting to spend more while the other was reluctant to. Eventually, their disagreements broke the company, and they went their separate ways shortly after I left. I later discovered that the brother that spent money so freely (and not in a particularly good way) is still working in construction at the age of sixty-six. The brother that practiced financial restraint, on the other hand, is now retired, owns around thirty acres of land on a nice lake, and gets to see his grandkids every week.

    It's a tale of two lives; two people cut from the same cloth, who had two different financial philosophies. One created this ultimate dream life, and the other one still has yet to. Most of us long for the joys of financial freedom and regaining control over our own time, but don't realize that we can obtain those things by adjusting our mindset and reprogramming our habits. How we manage our money is on us, and it's important to not make excuses for ourselves. And if you've struggled with financial hardship, you must learn the lessons that poverty teaches you, or else history will likely repeat itself and you likely won't ever be able to build the life of your dreams. Know that those things you desire are in fact possible, but *it's all on you*. Let that fact inspire rather than intimidate you.

Takeaways

- *The Fundamentals of Wealth.* Most of us are not taught financial literacy. But financial literacy is certainly not just for the experts; it's crucial for *everyone* to learn these fundamentals to live a financially healthy life. It ultimately comes down to learning how to properly manage your money so you can make wise decisions that will allow you to go on to create generational wealth.
- *The Basics.* Getting started on your journey to financial literacy isn't as daunting as you might think. The fundamentals are as easy as 1, 2, 3: all you need to do to get the ball rolling is (1) take stock of your assets and liabilities; (2) create a healthy budget; and (3) determine your magic number. Once these building blocks are established and you are able to get yourself to a more stable place, you can work on adding to your cash flow through investments and other opportunities to take your goals to new heights.

Chapter 8

Investing

"Construction is like a symphony. Each worker and team is an essential instrument, and the project manager is the conductor. Just as musicians must harmonize their efforts to create a beautiful piece of music, construction teams must coordinate and communicate effectively to build a successful project. The result is a masterpiece that stands the test of time, just as a symphony does when performed with precision and teamwork."

Sure, mastering the basics of wealth can give your life a little glow-up, but if you want the full VIP experience? Enter: passive income. Investing is like the cool cousin of traditional jobs – it's the ticket out of those "Oops, this isn't what I signed up for" career paths and into the world of generational wealth.

How to Mint Your Own Money

Remember those time lessons we chatted about? First off, figure out what your precious hours are worth. Then, have a little heart-to-heart with yourself. Where are you now, and where's that dream destination? Tiny goals are cute and all, but don't forget to dream big. And while you're in this introspective mood, ponder on that age-old 9-to-5 grind. Is that really the life-sized hamster wheel you want? If you're here, you're probably already side-eyeing the status quo. Good for you! Curiosity might've killed the cat, but it's your golden ticket to change, even when it feels like you're trying to turn a cruise ship.

Now, don't you dare underestimate the power of investing. It's like having a money tree that drops cash while you're dreaming of beaches. It's the ultimate level-up in the financial game, making those generational wealth dreams less fairy tale, more reality.

Feeling jittery about diving into the investment pool? Been there, done that. Every investment guru started as a rookie. To join the big leagues, you've got to take that first splash. With a bit of hustle and a dash of patience, you'll be lounging poolside, letting your money do the heavy lifting. Sure, it's a journey, but oh boy, the view from the top? Priceless.

Use your knowledge, skill sets, and talents to your advantage when making investment decisions. If you also come from a background in construction, real estate is an excellent option—even if you're not doing the construction work yourself, you understand the business, can understand values, and will be better positioned to identify bullshitters than others might be.

A great deal of millionaires are in the real estate industry due to the multitude of options to create cash flow, take advantage of tax incentives, and ultimately increase net worth. And you don't have to worry about doing everything yourself—all you need to get started is to partner up with the right people. Don't sleep on these opportunities! Your unique talents, whatever they may be, can be even more lucrative when you open your mind to all that you're capable of.

A Wealthy Mindset: Get Rich for Certain

"Sustainable construction is like planting a tree. It takes time and effort, but it provides benefits for generations to come."

Our mindset and attitudes are truly crucial to creating the lives we want to live. A great deal of it relates back to the scarcity versus abundance mindset. But at least when it comes to creating wealth, it's important to have some perspective on your goals and the logistics of achieving them.

KENT A KIESS

Part of having a wealthy mindset, which is essential to maintain to create and enjoy wealth, is having patience. Be realistic as to your goals, changes don't happen overnight. While creating wealth can be easy once you have the right tools, being your understanding of the fundamentals of time, health, and wealth, it still does take some work and thorough strategizing on your part.

A lot of investment opportunities, in particular those in real estate, are a slow game. But what's important is that it's a *sure* game. If you do things right, real estate investments *will* make you money. It's wise to be wary of "get rich quick" schemes. Instead, do yourself a favor and change your mindset to "get rich for certain." Future you will thank you for the generational wealth you created by being measured and ultimately, financially responsible.

Imagine! You've worked in construction all your life; now real estate is going to work for you! You might think investing in such a way is a long game, but five years goes by like that. While you're patiently waiting for investment opportunities to pay off, continue to make your money in those traditional ways that are familiar to you but remember to consider whether or not you're being cheated by your nine to five, and work to correct those issues. Trust that while you're hard at work, by playing the long game of investing, your money is working for you behind the scenes, and it will eventually pay off. And then a snowball effect can happen—

once you get your money back and then some, you can put it right back to work for you. It's like a conveyor belt that keeps producing income. This is how you create more wealth, but that cannot occur if you're caught up in short term gains and become frustrated when you don't see the fruits of your investments immediately.

Timing Your Investments

Time also comes into play with investment in that you must be cognizant of when to take action and when to hold off for better opportunities. Yes, there is some luck involved; my family often says that I'm blessed with good luck, be it by winning raffles, a couple bucks from scratch cards, or with lucrative investment opportunities. But I truly believe that most of the time, we create our own luck through maintaining the proper mindset. Think of people that win the lottery, but then go on to rapidly and foolishly spend their winnings and let it go to waste. Situations like this are unfortunate results of financial illiteracy, and you know better than that. And despite the success I've had with investing, I didn't hit it out of the park immediately—but that's just part of the process.

Part of creating your own luck and playing the long game of investing is timing, and timing the market. You have to do your due diligence to ensure you're investing efficiently. You'll see that there are "peaks" and "valleys" when it comes to investing, and when you're at the peak, you have to hold back and recognize that the timing is simply not right for what you want to achieve. Instead, be patient and wait for the valley. Yes, that is right I didn't confuse the two. A great quote by Nathan Rothschild is " when there is blood in the streets buy property".

"Creative Cash" by Bill Ham, in collaboration with Jake Stenziano and Gino Barbaro, reveals the hidden financing strategies that can empower individuals to invest in multifamily real estate without the need for traditional bank loans or substantial upfront capital. Ham shares his story of acquiring 400 units without setting foot in a bank and provides a step-by-step guide.

Through doing your due diligence to educate yourself before making investment decisions, you'll learn how the peaks and valleys are not the same for every investment opportunity. Each class of investments is unique and dependent on the ebbs and flows of the economy. When you do your homework on this and position yourself to make the best possible decisions for your personal goals, you're going to make *so much freaking money.*

I once heard from a very successful investor that no deal is ever found, but rather, it's created. To create investment opportunities such as those in real estate, assess the market, see what's available, and time your actions accordingly. But then, you may have to get a little creative when it comes to obtaining the money needed to partake in that opportunity.

You don't have to have a license or be a pro to get started—anyone can do this. You don't have to already be wealthy or have the right connections to create wealth; in my case, I didn't have a wealthy family or rich friends to embark on investment opportunities with. At one point in my life, I was down to my last dollar, not knowing what was going to happen next.

There are multiple avenues you can take, such as using the bank as leverage, or simply by working to gain trust with other investors. Trust is an important component of investing, as to be expected when people's money is on the line and in the hands of someone that may be a complete stranger. When building your network and working to gain trust from other investors, you may need to invite someone for a drink or dinner to get to know each other better and understand each other's financial philosophies and goals. It's all part of being financially responsible with your hard-earned money.

Do your due diligence before jumping into an exciting new opportunity. And if you find that a potential investment partner's philosophies and goals are not aligned with your own, it's often best for both of you to forego that joint venture. Regardless of whether or not a particular opportunity will work out, it's still incredibly valuable to grow and nurture your network, especially as a beginner investor.

Often, even if an opportunity doesn't play out with a particular investor, they can introduce you to others that may be a good fit or can simply add value to your life by growing your network even further. Don't ever underestimate the value and power of networking—break out of that lone wolf, do-it-yourself mentality. The most successful investors know to seek out resources that can make their investment endeavors more efficient, because they value their time and understand how to use it wisely.

Pay Yourself First

When I was growing up, my mom and dad became involved in a multi-level marketing company. I remember how they set up a little warehouse in the garage where they held all the inventory before they attempted to sell it. They really thought they were going to become millionaires within a year or so. They worked so hard at it, but of course, it didn't play out like they thought it would.

Regardless, I know their intentions were good. One of the things that stuck out to me is how my mom and dad would say that the money that came from the endeavor was to be used to pay themselves first. I'm fairly sure a lot of that money went into their company in an attempt to save the business, but as I've recounted, that ultimately didn't work out either.

Despite the failure, the lesson of paying yourself first was an important one that I've carried with me to this day. It goes back to knowing your worth and setting a value on your time—how much do you want to pay yourself for your work?

For me, that number was $1,365 each for my wife and myself; that way, we could use that money to follow through on our strategy to pay into the whole life insurance. After five years of this, we created our own little bank that we could borrow from (and that's how I ended up funding my single-family residence in Memphis!).

When you master the art of paying yourself first and understand that whatever you make needs to be put somewhere that makes you money, you'll create better habits that allow for sustainable financial freedom.

Becoming Your Own Bank

The infinite banking strategy allows you to become your own bank. It entails the same processes actual banks use—you give the bank a dollar, and it turns that dollar into eight dollars by instantly lending it out. Know that the system is set up so that you can borrow against it and use that fact to your advantage. Remember that not all debts are bad; if you do it right, this perpetual (but good) debt will help you snowball that debt into millions and millions of dollars. There are several ways to go about this; it may even mean taking out a Whole life insurance policy, borrowing against it in order to put it towards assets as the policy grows over time, and setting up a payment structure to pay it back.

Do your due diligence to educate yourself as to all the options available to you and create a strategy and roadmap to reach your goals. The key to becoming your own bank, and in turn achieving financial freedom, is implementing your newfound knowledge of the fundamentals of wealth and finding a way to make your money a real asset that makes you even more money, and to truly put your money to work, so that you don't have to.

***

Embarking on your investment journey, and working towards becoming your own bank, can be nerve-wracking—most of us are used to the structure and predictability that comes with what we know and what we have been taught, usually something along the lines of a nine to five gig. I get it—I thought I would work in construction forever, then thought working as an educator instead would pay off financially, and was left feeling frustrated and ultimately lost when I realized those paths simply weren't going to allow me to live the kind of life I wanted to live.

Remember that you don't have to be stuck in your traditions if they're not serving you well; make sure to contextualize what you have been taught and form your own philosophies, and always learn from mistakes, whether they're your own or those of others, lest they be repeated. Value your precious time, health, and wealth by designing the life *you* want to live.

Takeaways

- *Get your mindset in check.* Part of having the right mindset, in particular a wealthy mindset, is recognizing the importance of patience and restraint. Creating wealth through investment opportunities is typically a long game. Don't be tempted to throw your arms up in frustration if you don't see returns within a few weeks or so; take a step back and look at the grand scheme of your financial strategies. Remember that get-rich-quick schemes are often too good to be true and are not the way to go about achieving financial freedom. *You want to get rich for certain.* Perhaps you'll have to check back on your investments in a year. Trust that real estate in particular is a long, but ultimately rewarding game.

- *Timing.* Speaking of timing—another part of tying in your newfound knowledge of time to your investment strategies is doing your homework. Do your due diligence to understand the ebbs and flows of the economy before making investment decisions, so that you can jump on opportunities during the valley's rather than the peaks. When you're measured in your decisions in this way, you'll ensure you're using your valuable time, energy, and resources efficiently. This is especially crucial for beginner investors—start your investment journey out on the right foot!
- *Pay yourself first.* You already know the importance of knowing your worth and acting on that knowledge accordingly. Determine that number, and when you do get returns on your investments, get into the habit of paying yourself first. This will help you stay aligned with your goals, stick to the strategy you've carefully developed, and ultimately, create *sustainable* financial freedom.
- *The Infinite Banking Strategy.* When you master good habits, you can work towards becoming your own bank—some might even call it the epitome of financial freedom. It comes down to using those habits to turn your money into a real asset. Don't be afraid of good debt! Good debt puts your money to work, and you don't want that money sitting idly while you run yourself

into the ground chasing some idea, perhaps derived from your traditions, that may not be realistic.
- *A Blueprint for Construction Workers.* Chances are many of you reading this come from one of my industries. If you're overwhelmed with your newfound knowledge and don't know where to begin, here's a simple guide to consider:

1. Set up a financial team (and I recommend they are NOT family members, spouses, etc.). CPA, bookkeeper, lawyer, business coach, etc.
2. *Set up an LLC.* When you're self-employed, a business owner, or seeking to create a company, creating a formal business entity such as an LLC is a great place to start. Being your own boss is a wonderful feeling—just make sure you're keeping yourself organized and protected, and that you don't miss out on financial benefits such as tax incentives.
3. *Apply your knowledge and employ good habits.* Make sure you have a firm grasp on assets and liabilities and good debts and bad debts so you can start to spend your money wiser. When it's time, remember to pay yourself first, so you can start to invest your money so that it multiplies.

4. *Consider whole life insurance.* When you understand how the system is set up, you can make it work for you—an investment avenue such as whole life insurance can duplicate your efforts. Feel free to reach out to me if you need a hand here.
5. *Become an Accredited Investor* Do not hesitate to reach out to me on these 5 steps and we can go through them together. Send me an email: kent@beyondthetoolbelt.com

Chapter 9

KC-Investments

Successful real estate investing requires more than picking out a property, putting money down, and hoping for the best. Our team at KC-Investments helps investors build generational wealth by helping them invest in real estate syndications and other creative investments. The team has been investing in real estate since 2006, with a focus on active multi-family investing opportunities.

We offer our investors opportunities in real estate assets and the benefits associated with them by providing targeted investments that focus on intelligent and proven strategies, as well as the expertise, resources, and network necessary to achieve their financial goals.

Whether you're looking to diversify your portfolio, generate passive income, or ultimately build long-term wealth, this comprehensive guide is here to help you navigate the complexities of apartment investing with confidence. By the end of this chapter, you will have a solid foundation of knowledge in apartment investing, including an understanding of market trends, how to evaluate potential properties, financing options, and how to effectively manage your investment. We believe that everyone has the potential to become a successful apartment investor!

***

What is Multifamily Investing?

Overview, multifamily investing can be an attractive investment opportunity for those looking to generate passive income and build long-term wealth through real estate.

- Multifamily investing refers to the practice of investing in residential properties that have multiple units such as apartment complexes, townhouses, or condominiums. In this document, we use the term interchangeably with apartment investing. Multifamily properties are generally considered to be a type of commercial real estate investment.
- Multifamily investing can be done through various investment structures, such as direct ownership, joint

ventures, syndications, or through real estate investment trusts (REITs) or private equity funds that focus on multifamily properties.

- Investors can choose to invest in turnkey or value-add properties. The latter usually requires additional capital to improve the property's condition or amenities, but typically offer greater returns.
- Investors can also choose to invest in new developments, which is all about building new homes or apartments.

Why Invest in Apartments?

Overall, investing in apartments can be an excellent option for investors looking for **stable income**, **diversification**, **potential capital appreciation**, **ease of management**, and **tax advantages**. However, as with any investment, it is important to conduct thorough research and due diligence before making any investment decisions.

There are several reasons why investing in apartments can be a lucrative investment opportunity.

- Multifamily investing can be an attractive investment option for several reasons. For example, multifamily properties can generate a steady stream of rental

income from multiple units, which can provide investors with stable and predictable cash flow. Additionally, multifamily properties may be less volatile than other types of commercial real estate investments, such as office or retail properties, as there is always a demand for affordable housing.
- Investors in multifamily properties can also benefit from the economies of scale that come with owning multiple units in one property. This can help to reduce overall expenses and increase profitability.
- Apartments offer a relatively stable source of **income** as rental properties, with consistent cash flow and regular rental payments from tenants. This is particularly true for well-located apartments in high demand areas where the vacancy rates are low.
- Apartments provide an opportunity for investors to diversify their portfolio. Unlike other asset classes such as stocks or bonds, apartments are a physical asset, which can provide a hedge against **inflation** and market **volatility**.
- Apartments can offer a potential for **capital appreciation**. As the population continues to grow and demand for housing increases, **the value of well-located apartments** in desirable areas is likely to increase over time, providing a significant return on investment.

- Apartments are often easier to manage compared to other real estate assets. With a **professional property management company in place**, apartment owners can delegate most of the day-to-day responsibilities of managing the property to experienced professionals, freeing up time to focus on other investment opportunities.
- Apartments can offer **tax advantages for investor**s. Through depreciation, mortgage interest deductions, and other tax benefits, apartment owners can reduce their taxable income, thereby increasing their after-tax cash flow.

Should I Invest Through Syndication?

Overall: Investing in apartment building syndications can offer potential rental income and property value growth. Evaluate your investment goals and risk tolerance, research the syndication team's expertise, and conduct thorough due diligence on the property and market. Understand the investment structure, deal terms, and property management strategy. Consider how the investment aligns with your portfolio diversification. Legal and financial advice is crucial to comprehend tax implications and suitability. Recognize the long-term commitment and illiquidity of real estate investments. While this opportunity can be profitable, carefully weigh the risks and rewards before deciding.

Investing through a syndication that involves apartment buildings can be a potentially lucrative opportunity, but like any investment, it comes with risks and considerations that you should carefully evaluate. Here are some factors to consider before making a decision:

Investment Goals: Clarify your investment objectives. Are you seeking a stable income, capital appreciation, or a combination of both? Apartment buildings can provide regular rental income and potential for property value appreciation.

1. Risk Tolerance: Real estate investments, including apartment buildings, carry inherent risks such as market fluctuations, economic downturns, and property management challenges. Assess your risk tolerance before committing to such an investment.
2. Syndication Expertise: Research the syndication team's experience, track record, and reputation. A skilled and knowledgeable team can help navigate challenges and maximize returns.
3. Due Diligence: Thoroughly investigate the property and syndication team. Understand the property's location,

market trends, potential for rental income, expenses, and the overall business plan.
4. Investment Structure: Understand how the syndication is structured. You might be a passive investor with limited control over management decisions. Make sure you're comfortable with this level of involvement.
5. Deal Terms: Review the terms of the investment, including the distribution of profits, fees, preferred returns, and exit strategies. Ensure these terms align with your financial goals.
6. Market Analysis: Evaluate the local real estate market where the apartment building is located. A strong and growing market could enhance the potential for appreciation and rental income.
7. Property Management: The success of apartment investments often relies on effective property management. Assess the management team's capabilities and strategies for tenant retention and property maintenance.
8. Diversification: Consider how investing in apartment buildings fits into your overall investment portfolio. Diversification across asset classes can help mitigate risks.
9. Exit Strategy: Understand the syndication's exit plan. How and when do they plan to sell or refinance the

property? A clear exit strategy is essential for realizing your investment gains.
10. Legal and Financial Advice: Consult with legal and financial professionals who specialize in real estate investments. They can help you understand the legal aspects, tax implications, and overall suitability of the investment.
11. Long-Term Commitment: Real estate investments, especially in apartment buildings, are often illiquid and require a longer investment horizon. Be prepared for a longer commitment compared to more liquid investments like stocks.

What Should a Good Investment Strategy Look Like?

There is no silver bullet when it comes to investment strategy. A good investment strategy is one that takes care of your specific goals, needs and risk appetite. Here, we can provide some general principles of investing that can be helpful for investors to consider:

- Define your investment goals: Before making any investments, it is essential to determine your investment goals, such as your risk tolerance, time

horizon, and expected returns. This helps to align your investment strategy with your financial objectives.
- Diversify your portfolio: Diversification is key to reducing investment risk. By spreading investments across different asset classes and securities, you can mitigate the risk of losing all your investments in one area.
- Invest for the long term: Investing for the long term helps to reduce the impact of short-term market volatility and allows investments to compound over time.
- Keep costs low: Investment fees, transaction costs, and taxes can significantly reduce your investment returns over time. It's important to choose low-cost investments and consider tax-efficient investment strategies to maximize your returns.
- Monitor and review your investments: Regular monitoring and reviewing your investment portfolio helps to ensure that your investment strategy remains aligned with your goals and objectives. This allows you to make any necessary adjustments to your investments over time.

These principles are a good starting point for investors to develop their investment strategy. However, it's important to note that individual circumstances and goals can vary, and it's always advisable to seek professional financial advice before making any investment decisions.

Why invest with KC-Investments?

Successful real estate investing requires more than picking out a property, putting money down and hoping for the best. Our Team at **KC-Investments**, will help you build **generational wealth** for your family, and we do so through helping you invest in real estate syndications (group investing). The team has been investing in real estate since 2006; with a focus on active multi-family investing opportunities.

KC-Investments focuses on emerging and growth markets across the US. We conduct extensive market research to first identify our markets, and then deep dive to find sub-markets/ neighborhoods that cater to our strict selection criteria.

Once we identify our target markets, we work to grow our team and partnerships in those markets.

Currently we are very active in **the Arizona**, **Ohio** and **Texas markets** but we are constantly evaluating different markets and looking for opportunities.

These markets also offer diverse and growing economies, which can provide opportunities for both cash flow and long-term appreciation. As with any investment, it is important to conduct thorough research and due diligence before making a decision.

What Are Our Criteria When Choosing the Market? Metrics?

Some common metrics that KC-Investments considers when evaluating real estate markets include:

- population growth,
- job growth and diversity
- median household income
- rental rates
- vacancy rates
- housing affordability
- crime rates
- local regulations

These factors can help provide insight into the overall economic health and demand for housing in a given market. It's important to note that different investors may prioritize different metrics depending on their investment goals and strategy.

What is the minimum investment amount?

- These are deal dependent. Usually they vary between $50K - $100K minimum. However, talk to us if you have special needs.

What Are the Typical Returns on Investment?

Overview: The Internal Rate of Return (IRR) is a measure of the profitability of an investment or project over time. It represents the rate at which the initial investment amount is earned back. Cash on Cash (CoC) return is the percentage of money received on the initial investment. It measures the investor's return on their invested amount. Preferred Return is a structure in real estate investing where a specific group of investors is guaranteed a fixed return before other investors receive any profits. It provides a fixed annual return and reduces the risk for investors. Evaluating investment opportunities and associated risks is crucial before committing funds.

Returns vary by the market cycle, the location, the asset class, and the deal itself. Typical returns are in the mid to high teens.

- **IRR** stands for Internal Rate of Return. It is a way to calculate the profitability of an investment or project over time.

In simpler terms, IRR is the rate at which the investment earns back the initial amount of money put into it.

BEYOND THE TOOL BELT

For example, if you invest $100 into a project, and the IRR is 10%, then you can expect to earn $110 back from the project over a certain period of time.

- **Cash on Cash return** is the percentage of the money that an investor receives back on the amount they have invested. For example, if you invest $10,000 into a rental property and the Cash-on-Cash return is 8%, then you would receive $800 per year from the property.
- **Preferred Return:** Preferred Returns in Real Estate investing refer to a type of investment structure where a specific group of investors are guaranteed a fixed return on their investment before any profits are distributed to other investors.

For example, let's say a real estate developer is looking to raise $1 million to build a new apartment complex. They might offer preferred returns to a group of investors who provide $500,000 of the total investment. The developer promises to pay this group of investors a fixed annual return of 8% on their investment, which is paid out before any profits are distributed to other investors.

This means that if the apartment complex generates a profit of $300,000 in its first year, the preferred investors would receive $40,000 ($500,000 x 8%) in returns before any of the remaining profits are distributed to the other investors.

Preferred Returns can be an attractive investment option for investors who are seeking a fixed return and are willing to accept lower potential returns in exchange for reduced risk. However, it's important to note that not all real estate investments offer preferred returns, and investors should carefully evaluate the investment opportunity and associated risks before committing any funds.

What Is a Waterfall Structure in Investing?

Overview: A Waterfall structure in investing is a method of distributing profits among investors in a specific order. It is commonly used in partnerships like real estate deals or private equity funds. In this structure, profits are distributed according to predetermined terms. The first group to receive profits typically includes those who provided initial capital or have a guaranteed return. Subsequently, profits are distributed to other investors based on factors like additional investments or assumed risk. By using a Waterfall structure, investors can align incentives and minimize conflicts by establishing clear rules for profit distribution.

- A Waterfall structure is a way of distributing profits among different investors in a particular order. It is

BEYOND THE TOOL BELT

commonly used in investment partnerships, such as real estate deals or private equity funds.

- In a Waterfall structure, profits are distributed to investors in a specific sequence or "waterfall" based on the terms of the agreement. The first group of investors to receive a share of the profits is usually the ones who have provided the initial capital or have been promised a certain return on their investment, such as preferred investors.
- After that, the remaining profits are distributed to other investors in a predetermined order, such as those who have invested more money or those who have taken on more risk.
- For example, in a real estate investment, the Waterfall structure may dictate that the first 8% of profits go to preferred investors, followed by a certain percentage to other investors who have provided additional funding, and then the remaining profits to the general partner or sponsor of the investment.
- By using a Waterfall structure, investors can agree in advance on how profits will be distributed, which can help to align incentives and reduce conflicts between different parties.

What Is the Typical Hold Period?

Overview: the typical hold period for a Multifamily Real Estate investment can vary based on the individual investment's specific circumstances and the investor's overall investment strategy.

- The typical hold period for a Real Estate investment in Multifamily properties can vary depending on several factors, such as the location, property type, investment strategy, and market conditions. However, in general, most Multifamily real estate investors aim to hold their investments for a minimum of 3 to 5 years.
- During this hold period, investors may focus on increasing the property's value by implementing various strategies, such as improving the property's condition, increasing occupancy rates, and raising rental rates. Once the property has reached its full potential and the investor has achieved their investment goals, they may choose to sell the property for a profit.
- The decision to hold or sell a Multifamily property ultimately depends on various factors, such as the investor's financial goals, the property's performance, and the current market conditions. Some investors may choose to hold the property for a more extended period, while others may sell the property earlier to take

advantage of market trends or to invest in other opportunities.

What is a PPM?

Overview: It's important to note that the contents and specific details of a PPM can vary depending on the syndication and the preferences of the syndicator. Therefore, it is advisable to carefully review the specific PPM of a particular real estate deal to gain a comprehensive understanding of the investment opportunity and its terms.

- A PPM, or Private Placement Memorandum, is a legal document used in real estate syndication deals, including multifamily syndication. It serves as an offering document that provides detailed information about the investment opportunity to potential investors.
- The PPM is prepared by the syndicator (the entity or individuals leading the syndication) and is typically reviewed by legal professionals. It contains important information about the investment, including the property details, business plan, financial projections, risks involved, terms of the investment, and the syndication structure.
- The purpose of the PPM is to disclose all relevant information to potential investors so that they can make

an informed decision about whether to invest in the syndication. It ensures compliance with securities laws and regulations by providing full disclosure of the risks and terms associated with the investment.
- Investors typically review the PPM to understand the investment opportunity, evaluate the financial projections, assess the risks, and make an informed decision about whether to participate in the syndication. It is crucial for potential investors to thoroughly review the PPM and consult with legal, financial, and tax advisors to fully understand the terms and risks associated with the investment.

How Is the Asset Protected? Hurricane, Flood, Etc...

Overview: KC-Investments consult with professionals, such as insurance agents, property managers, and risk management specialists, to develop a comprehensive risk mitigation strategy tailored to the specific property and the potential hazards it may face.

Protecting real estate assets from natural disasters like hurricanes, floods, and other hazards is a crucial consideration for property owners. Here are some measures commonly taken to mitigate risks and safeguard real estate assets:

1. Insurance Coverage: Adequate insurance coverage is essential to protect real estate assets from potential damage caused by natural disasters. Property owners typically obtain property insurance policies that cover various perils, including windstorm/hurricane, flood, fire, and other hazards. It's important to review and understand the specific coverage terms, limits, deductibles, and exclusions in the insurance policy to ensure appropriate protection.
2. Risk Assessment and Mitigation Strategies: Property owners should conduct thorough risk assessments to identify potential vulnerabilities and develop mitigation strategies. This may involve assessing the property's location, susceptibility to natural disasters, and implementing appropriate structural reinforcements, such as hurricane-resistant windows, flood barriers, and secure roofing systems.
3. Building Codes and Regulations: Adhering to local building codes and regulations is crucial in constructing or renovating real estate assets. Building codes often include specific requirements related to resilience and protection against natural disasters. Compliance with these codes ensures that the property meets minimum

safety standards and enhances its ability to withstand potential hazards.

4. Emergency Preparedness and Response Plans: Developing and implementing emergency preparedness and response plans is vital for protecting real estate assets. These plans outline procedures for evacuation, securing the property, and minimizing potential damage before, during, and after a natural disaster. Training staff and tenants on these plans and conducting regular drills can help ensure a swift and coordinated response.

5. Property Maintenance and Inspections: Regular property maintenance and inspections are essential to identify and address any potential vulnerabilities or maintenance issues that could increase the property's susceptibility to natural disasters. This includes regular roof inspections, drainage system maintenance, and maintaining vegetation around the property to minimize potential risks.

6. Monitoring and Early Warning Systems: Utilizing monitoring systems and early warning technologies can provide advanced notice of potential natural disasters. These systems may include weather monitoring services, flood sensors, and other technological solutions that provide real-time information to take proactive measures in protecting the asset.

7. Offsite Data and Document Storage: Safeguarding critical data and documents related to the real estate asset is crucial. Maintaining offsite backups or utilizing cloud storage ensures that important records, lease agreements, insurance policies, and other essential documents are protected and easily accessible in case of damage to physical property.

Will There Be an LLC For the Property?

Yes. The property is held in an LLC to manage liability and easier compliance with SEC rulings. Usually, one property is held in one LLC to further limit cross-property impact.

We have Investor Updates

- Monthly Email
- Calls
- Semi-annual webinars
- Quick response by email or phone call
- Investor portal
- access to details for all investments
- Access to investment & tax documents
- Quarterly financials uploaded.

KENT A KIESS

***

If any of these intrigues you, I invite you to let KC-Investments help you build generational wealth through multifamily investments. With our expertise and experience in the real estate market, we can guide you through the process of identifying and acquiring lucrative multifamily properties. By investing in multifamily properties, you can tap into the potential for consistent cash flow, long-term appreciation, and tax advantages. Our team will assist you in conducting thorough market research, performing due diligence, structuring deals, and managing the properties. With our strategic approach and dedication to your financial success, KC-Investments is committed to helping you create a lasting legacy of wealth.

Conclusion

If you have made it to the end of this book, I commend you for taking the proactive first steps required to transform your life to be what you want it to be. Life really is what you make of it. That fact can either hold you back in fear, or it can empower you to construct the custom life of your dreams.

It all comes down to a few overarching concepts that touch numerous aspects of our lives. Our traditions, and the mindsets we develop as a result of them, ultimately shape our entire experience here on Earth, whether or not we can recognize it. Your mindset is everything—if you have developed one that you have discovered is holding you back from your desires, now is the time to adjust it and get yourself on the right track.

We don't have to be confined into the box we find ourselves in from our early circumstances. If you want out, just open the box and leave. *Be* the change. Sure, that's easier said than done, but you can't get anywhere if you're stuck in the trap of your own limiting mindset of scarcity, which tells you that a box is sealed when it really isn't. Let your desires guide you rather than your fears; chances are your desires are far more likely to take you where you want to be.

KENT A KIESS

Time, health, and wealth are all interconnected. In order to achieve your goals, in order to live that fulfilling life of your dreams, you must learn the principles that govern each of them. This invaluable knowledge is not always apparent to us, and sometimes we simply must take the initiative to seek out that knowledge ourselves, and to be proactive about making the changes we want in our lives. The only person that has that ultimate power is you—you are the artist, architect, designer, and construction worker tasked with the passion project that is your life.

Whatever you are going through in regard to your traditions, mindset, time, health, or wealth, remember that you are never alone. There are plenty of others out there who have walked the same path and have made mistakes so that you don't have to. If you think that investing in real estate could be a viable avenue to reach your goals, know that there are numerous options available to you that can allow you to come on over to where the grass is greener.

KC-Investments is one of those options—if you are seeking out like-minded individuals that understand where you come from culturally, traditionally, philosophically, or any combination thereof, *we are here as a resource to you.*

At the end of the day, generational wealth, and living a fulfilling life, are meant for everyone, not just the lucky ones. Never forget that you create your own luck. And above all,

BEYOND THE TOOL BELT

opening your mind to the potential of living your dreams will be what ultimately blesses you with that life.

KENT A KIESS

Inquiries

For inquiries, contact Kent Kiess at kent@beyondthetoolbelt.com or visit www.kc-investments.com for more information on our services and offerings.

Books and References

The following titles are mentioned throughout the book but thought it would be good to put them all here. You can also see a list of books that we recommend at:

www.kc-investments.com

Enjoy!

Rich Dad Poor Dad by Robert Kiyosaki
The Miracle Morning by Hal Elrod
The One Thing by Gary Keller
Who Stole my Pension by Robert Kiyosaki
Tax Free Wealth by Tom Wheelwright
Creative Cash by Bill Ham, Jake Stenziano and Gino Barbaro
Getting Things Done by David Allen

Made in United States
Orlando, FL
25 January 2024